# MAKING YOU TURN

# MAKING YOU TURN

Harkirat Iqbal

AMARYLLIS

AMARYLLIS

An imprint of Manjul Publishing House Pvt. Ltd.
• C-16, Sector 3, Noida, Uttar Pradesh 201301, India
Website: www.manjulindia.com
*Registered Office:*
• 10, Nishat Colony, Bhopal 462 003 – India
*Distribution Centres*
Ahmedabad, Bengaluru, Bhopal, Kolkata, Chennai,
Hyderabad, Mumbai, New Delhi, Pune

*Making You Turn* by Harkirat Iqbal



This edition first published in India in 2024

**ISBN 978-93-5543-999-4**

Cover design by Harkirat
Illustrations by Iqbal

Printed and bound in India by Thomson Press (India) Ltd.

Dedicated

to

the Master

in

You

# From The Authors

**Making You Turn** is a book that maps your inner territory and provides tools of reliable navigation so that you stay on the right path while exploring this otherwise unfamiliar terrain.

This book promises to transform your life provided it is lived in true sense. We suggest you read it in a small group of like-minded friends. The discussions will bring refreshing understanding and sharing will enhance experiential depth.

---

www.thelifeschoolbhopal.org may help those seeking deeper understanding of what this book offers.

# Contents

# WHY THIS BOOK

# Chapter 1

# Why This Book

All of us have different priorities, goals, aspirations, ideas and views. But without a speck of doubt, there is one thing common to everyone – the desire to be happy.

And to be happy, we do all kinds of things – earning riches, scoring higher grades, getting promotions, finding a valentine, playing games and building relationships. Nobody makes a conscious effort to invite suffering in their lives. In that sense, every human action is fundamentally a quest for joy. Even though people leave no stone unturned in the pursuit of happiness, yet it remains mysteriously elusive. More so, for reasons not clear to us, happiness is always short lived while grief, which is always unsolicited, lingers like an affliction – sometimes persisting for a lifetime. No amount of reading, listening to audio-video discourses, making pilgrimages or austere compliance of scriptural preaching bring lasting relief. People, have grown so accustomed to this state of affairs, that suffering appears to be a natural phenomenon from which there is no escape. No wonder most of them do not make any effort to find a way out of this morass.

Our own life experience was not any different. Like everyone else, we learnt values, religious prescriptions, rituals, cultural ethos and also acquired livelihood skills to gain the competence necessary to become 'successful'. Remember 'successful' not 'joyful'. It seemed intuitively correct to postulate that undesirable life situations bring pain whereas favorable times make living pleasant. So, the swing of the pendulum between these two extremes seemed inevitable. The deep grooves of conditioning influenced all our thinking and doing. Any idea of approaching life situations from a new point of view did not appeal. The futility of the traditional means in seeking joy or firewalling sorrows was not easy to recognize. The voice of truth, low and soft as it is, was never heard in the din of achieving goals and becoming something.

But providence brought about certain personal and professional circumstances which provided an opportunity to explore the subject of joyful living. We read books and listened to innumerable discourses by distinguished men. It was very instructive but not transformative. To deep dive we felt the need to create a platform where thoughts and emotions could be shared with likeminded people. With some effort, a small group of families who trusted each other, was formed. We began meeting on regular basis. Together we studied the subject, discussed and practiced. Close relationship rooted in mutual confidence between the group members facilitated a warm sharing of personal experiences during these get-togethers. It was a teaching-learning-teaching cycle which removed doubts, clarified concepts and brought a new depth in experiential learning. This collective endeavor helped everyone to understand the science of life energy and the art of managing it. In this process the importance of unlearning much of what is learnt through organized social, educational and cultural system was revealed. It gradually became clear to us that a happy and fulfilling life is a not a matter of destiny, but that of choices that we make.

The affirmative impact of these discussions on the quality of life was recognized by everyone in the group. If few simple, though not necessarily easy, things could transform our lives, they surely hold promise for others too. It is said that the wealth of such experiential understanding is quickly lost if not sufficiently shared. We observed that much more is added to the treasure when the depth and extent of sharing increases. A strong urge to share stirred us into writing this book. It is our humble effort to reach out to more people in the hope that they will also benefit from it.

There is no dearth of prescriptions in the market which claim to offer a genuine panacea for all kinds of suffering. It is pointless to argue which one is more effective. Preaching or prescriptions of scriptural or academic authorities may help but they do not bring sustained equanimity. Happiness is not an outcome of any intellectual exercise or any worldly pursuit. It is existential in nature and comes from somewhere within us. Therefore it is important to know what constitutes our 'inner world' and understand the principles that govern their functioning. This knowledge can then be used to gain skills necessary for creating a peaceful and joyful state of being. Such learning should be validated by our daily experiences without taking recourse to any philosophical, mystical or religious notions. It is quite similar to the study of physiotherapy. If the understanding of the anatomy of muscles and joints is correct, effective physical exercises that will keep the body in good shape can be designed.

This book is a manual which explains the functioning of the control mechanisms of the mind-body vehicle. After studying these in some detail, we need to put in sufficient practice to gain proficiency in operating them. The degree of expertise so gained will help us in consciously improving the quality of our lives. It enables us to steer life amidst the usual traffic of tragedies, comedies, successes and failures. But reading and understanding the text of this book will not be enough – it has to be lived earnestly if you intend to experience profound transformation. In our everyday lives, many moments arise that offer opportunity to understand the way life forces work and also for practicing techniques that help us in controlling them. By recognizing and using these moments of opportunity, we gain the proficiency necessary for leading a peaceful and joyful life.

In a way, it is quiet similar to the way we learn driving. Studying the manual of a car does not make anyone a skilled driver; it is possible if driving is seriously practiced. Before actually starting to drive, we learn the functions of steering, ignition and various pedals. Initially, as you take charge of the wheel and start off, controlling the car and using the brake, gear and the clutch seems formidable. But it does not take long to overcome these early difficulties of coordination. Usually, driving lessons start in an open ground. Soon, you take to busy roads and gradually move to highways. A time comes when chatting with other passengers, listening to music and looking around while driving takes no extra effort. Maneuvering through crowds, lanes and crossings becomes as easy as driving in an open ground. The driver and the driven seamlessly become one. You are the master of the car. When it comes to this body-mind vehicle the approach is quite similar. The first step is to understand the control features and then to practice using them to make it function smoothly. This essentially means that you can choose to drive it – away from sorrows and towards the much desired happiness. This is how we master our life. We cease to be at the mercy of others – people or things or situations – for peace, joy and fulfillment.

What does the title of this book **"Making You Turn"** mean? It means to turn our attention away from external distractions (or attractions) and bring it upon what is happening within. The effect of a stimulus, received through sense organs, depends less on its contents and more on how it is processed. A deep understanding of this simple fact can make you realize experientially that happiness is not an object to be pursued, but an outcome of mastering our inner world. Unlearning is a significant part of a process involving learning of this kind. It is necessary to drop the baggage of preconceived notions, beliefs and other patterns deeply etched in the mind. So, what is essential for 'making you turn', so that joyful living may be experienced? The answer is simple: Make the right choice. If you don't, even simple things will not be easy to achieve – much like a man who wants sunlight in the room but chooses to keep the windows closed. Who should be blamed when he complains about the darkness?

For most of us, the world within is an uncharted territory. Our upbringing, training, education and conditioning hold us back so firmly that we make no attempt to seriously explore it. The common belief that this journey can be undertaken only by renouncing social and familial responsibilities dissuade us further. In these conditions, making a right choice becomes even more challenging. This book attempts to introduce navigational tools essential for making the right choices so that you take the much needed 'U-turn' along with necessary shift in the 'gear'. These tools will assist you to drive life quietly amidst the maddening chaos of traffic outside. Sorrows appear, but will pass more like roadside trees. The daily situations are like potholes that can easily be driven around. You learn to leave anger, jealousy, regrets and shames behind just like the fields, huts and shops which are left behind as you drive by. You see them all but do not carry any of them along on the ride. When you take this 'U-turn', a fundamental shift in perspective takes place. You stop depending on the fulfillment of wants in order to experience joy. The most challenging and threatening life situation will not overwhelm anymore. You become silent, and suddenly, the music of life becomes audible.

An experiential understanding of the science and the art of joyful living makes you the master of your inner world. Once that happens, you hold the key to the door of the eternal 'spring of joy within'. You can now unlock it at your own sweet will.

# THE SPACE WITHIN

## Part One

## Chapter 2

# THE SPACE WITHIN

## Part One

The existence of a 'Spring of Joy Within' looks doubtful when we see so much suffering in the world. It appears to be more of a fiction than a fact. If it is not a figment of imagination or a part of some mythological lore, why do people invariably fail to reach it? What keeps this spring out of their reach?

Most of us remember our childhood with a sense of relish. A child frolics innocently and engages spontaneously with the world. There is freedom from both the burden of the past and the fear of an uncertain future. There are neither any attachments nor expectations. It is suffused with a sense of wonder at everything – even the most ordinary. Life is ruled by the heart and the mind works just enough to keep the physical body safe. A child does not judge people, hold grudges or enter into competition with those around. But as we grow up the spontaneous joy of childhood inevitably fades away. Life, for the most part, becomes a fountainhead of sorrow in which we lurch from one pain to another. It is amazing that childhood does not require any formal training or acquisition of knowledge or skills in order to be joyful. It is a natural state, which does not subsist as we move away from the shores of infancy. It is tragic to see human life begin in a state of absolute joy and end up in a cesspool of suffering.

The attempts to understand suffering and to get rid of it are as old as human history. The underlying theme in Nirvana of Buddha, Kaivalya of Mahavira, Salvation of Jesus, Mukti of Nanak or Moksha of Krishna is the same – to end the suffering. They spoke, in their own unique way, about the same unconditional joy we all seek but which remains elusive in everyday life experience.

People make all kinds of efforts to keep pain away and snatch few moments of happiness. However all these pursuits end repeatedly in the pits of grief. The travelogue of human journey offers a vivid description of the tragic failure of our endeavors to seek fulfillment. They make for a sad reading. Clearly, men have traversed the wrong path – a path that failed to fulfill its promise of bringing joy. But people are unable to appreciate this fact because cultural conditioning, familial training and societal inhibitions draw blinds over their eyes. To look at the world outside for solution to our sorrows is a common approach. There are enough players in the market who exploit this tendency to attract the unhappy souls. Most of them do it for commercial reasons and few others may have been inspired by religious bigotry. "There must be good reason for having so many followers. Not all of them can be mistaken" is heard very often. People make such statements believing that a man who has large following must be propagating something valuable. Tragically, deeply etched patterns of thinking become the very raison d'être for the trust and veneration in these men. Since it is not easy to recognize our conditioning, the inspiration necessary to question the prevailing ways of living and thinking becomes difficult to come.

To understand what goes wrong as we move from childhood to old age, it is essential to study in some detail this complex organism called human being. There are two ways of understanding its functioning. One is primarily biological which includes the chemistry and physics of the physical body. Scientific experimentation and research is the foundation of this approach. All activities and experiences, whether physical or mental, are investigated and explained on the basis of well-defined properties of matter and energy. Subjects like physiology, psychology, neurology, biochemistry and genetics have emerged out of this approach. The other way of understanding human beings is purely experiential. In this approach the constituents of human existence are identified on the basis of what is experienced in everyday life. The functioning of these elements is then studied through close observation. An understanding of the reasons underlying our real-time experience emerges from such inspection. We begin to get an insight into what happens to us and why.

We intend to take this experiential approach in this book.

Very often people say, "There is a deep hurt **inside** me." or "I am peaceful **within**." By using the words **inside** and **within** they are trying to point towards a particular space which seems to hold immense significance in our life. What happens in this realm deeply affects our emotional well-being and mental state. It is therefore important to know what goes into the making of this space.

## The Space called 'Inside' or 'Within'

The following four elements comprise the 'inside':

i. Body
ii. Thoughts
iii. Emotions
iv. Energy

Some of us may find the term elements confusing. The Indian school of thought considers Earth, Water, Fire, Space and Air as the five fundamental elements that constitute the universe. However the purpose here is to bring the reader in touch with his daily personal experiences without referring to any established system of spirituality, whether it be philosophy enunciated in Indian Yoga, Japanese Zen, Chinese Chan or Tibetan Buddhism. Therefore the term 'element' used here has no relationship with what it may connote in the discourse of any theological schools.

At a more subtle level the body, thoughts and emotions are all energies. Einstein was the first to prove mathematically that matter and energy are indistinguishable because at quantum level they keep interchanging their forms. The equation $E = mc^2$ states that the amount of energy possessed by an object is equal to its mass multiplied by the square of the speed of light. Since the speed of light is incredibly high, almost 300,000 km/sec, a small amount of mass contains enormous amount of energy. In that sense, these four different elements can be reduced to one, i.e. energy. However it would not be possible to understand this space unless we discuss these four elements separately.

## 1. Body

Body, the first element, is the vehicle for the other three. It is the interface between the outside and the inside. The sense organs render the outside world on the mind-screen making experiencing possible. It is therefore, in contact with both realms. The body which is seemingly the outside is thus very much a part of the inside. In that sense, this division of inside and outside is artificial.

The physical occurrence of experiences can be explained in terms of psychological and physiological mechanisms in a living organism. The biological reasons of sensations felt through a complex system of nerves and the regulated release of innumerable chemicals (like serotonin, endorphins, oxytocin and adrenalin) are taught in every medical school. We know pain at only the physical level like the sting of a thorn, pangs of hunger or hurt of a wound. When the need of the body like – removing the thorn, eating a good meal and healing a wound is met – we experience pleasure. This feeling of pleasure at the level of the body is not the joy that we are looking for. We can go about doing our daily chores effortlessly if the body is in good condition. The body is healthy only if no specific part (i.e. organ) draws in your awareness. (We are overlooking certain medical conditions, like severe diabetes, in which nerve endings stop working and the person doesn't feel any pain when the affected part is physically hurt). Imagine a headache or mosquito bite. It can absorb your attention to such an extent that the rest of the world ceases to exist. It is therefore important to keep the body in a pleasant state otherwise it would not be possible to focus attention on other three elements.

Indian traditions consider body the sacred temple of God. The governing principle for keeping the body in good order is moderation. Both excess and excessive restraint whether of eating, drinking or exercising will cause sickness.

## 2. Thoughts

The dictionary meaning of thought is:

*"An idea, plan, opinion, picture etc. that is formed in your mind."*

It is something you think of. Thoughts appear in large numbers. Some studies claim that some 60,000 thoughts occur in 24 hours. Interestingly, nobody learns how to create these thoughts or to think; it comes naturally to us. Why does a particular thought occur at a given point in time is not clearly known although there are theories that make attempts to explain it. However, we have the capacity to use them for definite purposes, like doing scientific research or completing school homework. This faculty has helped men make numerous discoveries and inventions.

We all know that thoughts keep surfacing on their own and this constant flow can be a source of great misery to us. That be so is it possible at least to stop thinking particular thoughts?

*Jhumroo once went to a monastery to seek guidance from the Master. "All kinds of thoughts keep bothering me the entire day. I want to dispel them so that there is peace of mind. Please help me do it?" He said. "Tell me a thought you want to dispel," said the Master. "The thought of my wife, who has left me for another man." said Jhumroo. "That is simple," said the Master, "Sit in that corner and tell your mind not to think of her."*

*Jhumroo struggled not to think. The harder he tried the bigger the images of his ex-wife and her lover grew. Exhausted he went back to the Master in the evening and narrated his predicament. "You cannot force your mind not to think about a particular object." said the Master, "So don't make an effort to do that. Relax. Just watch the thoughts come. Anything that comes will always go away. So will these thoughts. That is the only way."*

This story enunciates a fundamental principle:

*A thought cannot be forced to disappear. Give it the freedom to come, watch as if it is a floating cloud. With that watching it will disperse on its own.*

People who do not understand this fundamental truth make naïve statements like "Don't think like that" or "Don't let such thoughts come to you". This is advising them to control thoughts – something that does not work. In the process of controlling, we end up either suppressing or brushing them away. We will see later in the chapter how this resistance and avoidance creates more problems than solving any.

## The flow of thoughts

Even when you are not speaking, a constant chattering goes on within. There is a voice inside which talks constantly – usually about past regrets and future worries. It counsels, cautions, offers solace and even reprimands you. It is as if a person, who babbles relentlessly, is living inside. We are so used to it that an objective assessment of its impact on the quality of our life has become impossible.

When the doorbell rings on a Sunday afternoon, the voice inside your head begins to curse the guest "Why do people come unannounced to ruin a holiday? I am not going to open the door." The voice inside expresses satisfaction when the visitor leaves without meeting you. Later when you discover that it was your fiancée who came to give a surprise, the same voice articulates a deep regret "Oh God! Why was I so lazy?"

While reading this book silently, you can easily hear someone inside speaking out the words one by one and forming the whole sentence. You are not reading it aloud, yet you, hear the words inside. That is the same voice at work within. To experience it differently, close your eyes right now and say "God help me" without uttering any sound. Were you able to hear it?

You will note that whether the subject is frivolous or serious, both speaking and listening goes on simultaneously. If some fear, anxiety or desire begins to trouble, the voice becomes very active. It can engage in conjecturing, makes things look worse than they actually are or might argue in ways that makes you feel comfortable. Imagine your daughter who promised to call back home after reaching the destination she was travelling to. But she did not. You find her mobile is switched off. "What happened? Why is she unreachable? She has never done this before," says the voice. As your anxiety grows, you hear it say "Who should I call to locate her? Is she all right?" The situation can be nerve wracking when the fear that she might have been criminally assaulted arises in the mind. But all these stories that the voice conjures up are forgotten when she calls back "Sorry Mom, couldn't call earlier. The battery of my mobile went off." Instantly a sense of relief descends.

Who is it inside us who never stops talking? Whose voice is that? It is an integral part of our existence ever since we began to think. In fact, most of us identify ourselves with it and this identification is so absolute that we are unable to distinguish between this partner and our self. When he renders advice, anticipates, reminds, cribs or passes judgment on others, we construe it as our doing. When you think, "I will get up early and complete my homework", this is the partner inside speaking. When you rise late next morning, he admonishes "You should have finished the assignment before going to sleep?" Can you see the bluff? It was the partner who initially suggested that you complete the task next morning but later rebukes for not having completed it before going to bed the previous night. When the partner renders advice, anticipates, reminds, cribs or passes judgment on others, we consider it as our doing. Therefore blaming him feels like as if we are blaming ourselves. Many a times we hold others responsible even though the situation was actually created by him. We have no capacity to distinguish between what we construe as 'ourself' on one side and the partner on the other. The idea of the partner as a separate entity sounds weird and may even be incomprehensible to many of us.

All creative endeavors require thinking i.e. verbalizing the thoughts in an organized manner keeping the desired end in view. That is how we plan a vacation or execute a billion dollar project. Einstein used to set up an entire thought laboratory in which certain actions were conceived, listed mentally and their possible results noted. This capacity to think is responsible for great discoveries and inventions throughout the history of mankind. The partner in such situations play the role of a hero. But there are times when it chooses to play a villain. Recall the incident in which your daughter could not be contacted on mobile when the partner almost convinced you that a tragedy has struck her.

When the current problem is resolved, the partner is quick in bringing up a new one in an unending series. However careful observation will show that as soon as the partner becomes silent, a sense of peace descends on you. Such moments are short, few and far in-between. But there is a clear cause and effect relationship between the chatter stopping and the corresponding moments of tranquility. The inner voice is essentially a continuous flow of thoughts. It is nothing but incessant thinking – which most of the time keeps:

- Obsessing over imaginary or perceived threats
- Wondering what other people might be thinking about us
- Imagining response to past scenarios or future projections
- Playing out past hurts and resentments
- Enacting things yet to be done

This flow of thoughts continuously draws our attention. It depletes the energy store and therefore can be quiet exhausting.

The way inner voice affects us is vividly described by Sam Harris in his podcast titled 'The Veil of Thought' as follows:

*"When you sit down to meditate you will find yourself assailed by thoughts – thoughts about what you need to do in the day, thoughts about things that worry you, thoughts about things you want or don't want. The moment you attempt to pay attention to your breath or to the sound of the wind in the trees, you will meet your mind. And your mind is the most rambling, chaotic, needling, insulting, insufferable person you will ever meet. It is like having a maniac walk through the front door of your house and follow you from room to room and refuses to stop talking."*

A joyful life (some call it spiritual life) begins when you clearly perceive the partner as a separate entity. A new 'You' is born when identification with him comes to an end.

### 3. Emotions

Thoughts evoke emotions. Recall a past incident and see how it brings back the feelings associated with it. These could be painful or joyful depending on the way the event was perceived at the time of its happening. In fact thought-emotion-thought can become a vicious self-propagating cycle which can lead people to commit suicide in depression or murder in rage. The persistent flow of thoughts is also very tiring. They sap enormous amount of energy by causing memories and emotions to flare up continuously.

For the purpose of simplicity, we use the words 'emotion' and 'feeling' interchangeably. Though every emotion is a feeling, every feeling may not be an emotion. For example, thirst and hunger are feelings but not emotions. Thoughts appear in the field called mind, whereas emotions arise inside that part of us which is popularly called the heart. The head in our body is supposed to be the house of thoughts and the middle of the chest (where you keep your hand unconsciously while taking a vow of love), is the seat of emotions – the proverbial heart. Thoughts can remain private until verbalized, but emotions can be felt by others even without any vocal expression. They somehow get reflected in the persona and can be instinctively read. This has made possible a unique mode of communication called the body language. Anger, love, hatred and fear can be easily seen. A careful observer can also perceive the presence of shame, guilt and regret in another person.

We know, as explained earlier in this chapter, that thoughts cannot be wished away. But if left untouched, they float away and gradually disperse. The same applies to feelings. If you allow them to surface, while keeping a close watch on them, they weaken with the passage of time and finally disappear. In daily life, if we are not attentive enough, rising emotion can ensnare our awareness. The consequences can be really serious if people get overwhelmed by an emotional upsurge.

We handle feelings in three ways: Suppression, Expression and Escape.

- Suppression means to consciously push feelings aside, either by denial or simply overlooking them. Repression is another form of suppression which happens on a subconscious level and remains out of our awareness. For example a child abused in the early years may fail in relationships as an adult. He becomes distrusting of others not knowing that it is the outcome of the traumatic childhood events.
- Expression means to let the feeling manifest. It could be through verbalizing (like abusing, giving thanks) or physical action (like violence or embracing).
- Escape means to avoid. It could be in the form of ignoring, overlooking or distraction. Activities like drinking, shopping, watching TV or taking drugs also help people in avoiding feelings arising within.

All these methods push energy of the event into deep recesses of the psyche. When they get stoked, for whatever reasons, these events reappear on the mind-screen and bring back the emotions associated with it. People blame others when this process causes pain. They do not realize that it is happening because of an earlier suppression or repression or escape. They feel like an innocent victim of external causes although it was their own doing. By saying "He made me angry", "It scared me" we conveniently make other person or a thing responsible. All our inner disturbances belong to us. They are our own creation and nobody can actually be held accountable for them. Yet a significant part of human life is wasted in blaming others for causing them.

The following pictorial depiction helps in broadly understanding the connection between stimulus, memory, thoughts, chattering and emotions.

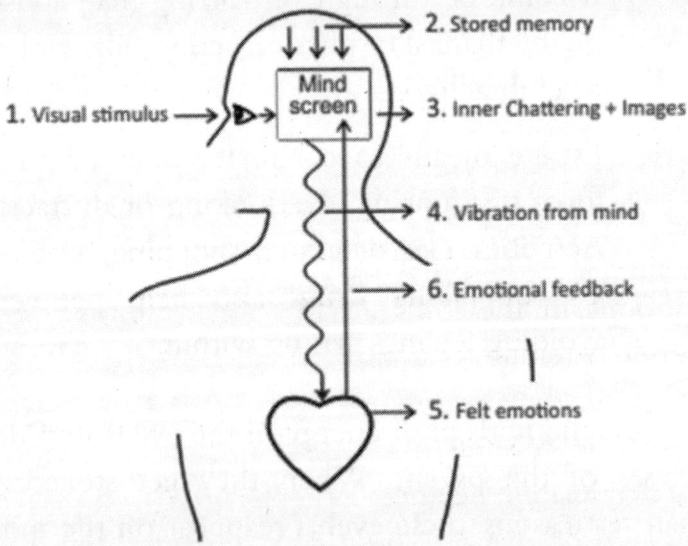


1. The visual stimulus is received through the eye.

2. The stored memory is activated.
3. The stimulus and the memory retrieved is mixed to produce chattering and images which appears on mind screen.
4. The vibrations from the mind reach the heart.
5. An emotion or mix of emotions is felt.
6. The mind receives emotional feedback from the heart which can further modify ongoing activity of mind.

### 4. Energy

Every movement in the physical world is made possible by the use of energy. In the same way, everything happening in our body-mind complex like walking, digesting, occurrence of an emotion or appearance of a thought, needs energy. That is why anxiety and stress are exhausting. The rush of thoughts and emotions in these mental states consumes a lot of energy. Attempt to control them tires them further and if one breaks down, the resulting fatigue would indeed be severe. In extreme distressful conditions like depression, the affected person experiences a very low level of energy. No amount of eating improves it because the calories provided by food do not give the kind of energy necessary to come out of such state. In fact depression is notorious for killing appetite.

Very often we feel a sudden surge of energy on winning a lottery or getting a high rank in the exam or defeating a national champion. It exhilarates, invigorates and appears to fill us up with new zeal. On the other hand we feel low on hearing that a loved one has died or discovering that a trusted friend has betrayed. People demonstrate amazing physical strength, not ordinarily seen in them, in certain threatening situations. It is similar to the courage that a wild buffalo sometimes demonstrates when its calf is attacked by a lion. This can be explained in terms of biological changes caused by the release of certain chemicals in the body which gives the strength necessary to do such a daring act. Undergoing this feeling of high or low can also be understood in terms of the flow of the life-force. When this flow is uninhibited one experiences a natural state of health and vitality. But if it is inhibited, you feel dejected and upset.

To measure the current status of energy flow, ask yourself a simple question:

"Am I Joyful?" or, "Am I feeling pleasant?"

Take your time to check and find what the answer is?

If your mind is quiet and serene, it means that the energy flow is sufficiently free; and if you are depressed the flow is blocked. If it stops altogether, life would come to an end. We experience joy and despair of different levels at different time each day. This means that energy flow changes over time. Obviously, there must be some system at work which blocks and unblocks the path. It would be useful to understand the structure of this system because whether we bloom or live in gloom depends on how it functions.

Suppose, you detest a person. One fine day while walking down a street, you see him approaching. It could be a friend who betrayed, or the girlfriend who ditched you for another man. You feel a slight tightening around the chest and abdomen. Instinctively you want to avoid him. This physiological change in the body is due to sudden restriction in the flow of energy. This is the state in which the heart is said to have partially closed. Now imagine another situation, in which you see a loved one on the street. This time something opens up inside and you may want to rush up to hug him. This means that the flow of energy has increased and the heart has opened up. These feelings (of hate and love in the two instances described above), are actually manifestations of the change in the energy flow effected by the nature of stimulus received. This energy is called *Shakti* in *Yoga*, Chi in Chinese and the spirit in the west. It is the life force which remains in play all the time. It has no relationship with age, gender or physical strength. Although it cannot make an otherwise physically weak person strong yet it makes him, what we commonly call, a 'spirited man'.

Those who drive know very well that if an object (be it a man, an animal or a simple obstruction) suddenly comes up on the road in front of the car, a sudden punch hits in the abdomen as you slam the brakes. In the same way, people feel butterflies while appearing before an interview board or while standing behind the podium to address the audience. Both these experiences, i.e. the punch or the fluttering sensation in the pit of your stomach is because of sudden closing of the heart causing restriction in the energy flow. Try recalling time you felt a wave of love or a rush of enthusiasm. It was nothing but experiencing a pleasant surge of energy. It is obvious that there is a direct relation between joyfulness and the extent to which the heart is open. Let us do the following exercise:

1. Sit comfortably and close your eyes. Release all tension in the body by simply watching different parts of it one by one for a minute.
2. Slowly, exhale as much as you can. Pull in your stomach to further empty the lungs. Now, let go of all tension. As the air rushes in to fill you up, visualize your heart as a flower whose petals are opening.

   Relax and release.
3. In the next inhalation tell yourself that no

matter what happens or has happened you will not let the heart close.

Relax and release.

Repeat steps 2 and 3 at least 8 to 10 times.

Be aware (Beware) of the thoughts. They will always pull you away on a different trip during this practice.

Remember, heart opens when we like a situation or person (e.g. when you see a loved one) and begins to close down when we dislike (e.g. when someone you detest is seen). Can we increase our likes and decrease our dislikes to keep the heart open? No, that is not possible by conscious effort. Every person has as many dislikes as the likes. They are two obverse sides of the same coin which cannot be separated. They cannot be eliminated but surely transcended – which means we can go beyond both so that, for all practical purposes, they do not become the underlying cause of any obstruction to the energy of stimulus passing through the system.

## The closing and opening of the Heart

Let us study the process which closes the heart in detail. The outside world comes in through our sense organs. It affects different people differently depending on how they process it. That is why a particular event can generate fear or anxiety in one person, but hope or contentment in another. This 'processing' happens as follows:

An object (be it a person or an incident), comes through a single sense or a combination of senses in the form of energy. Touch, smell or taste is the result of physical contact with an object whereas both sight and hearing is the result of waves of energy entering the body through eyes and the ears. All stimulus reach our brain through nerves and gets recorded in the memory system, wherefrom it can be retrieved as a thought in the future. For example while driving you see the buildings, traffic on the road, people on sidewalks and the surrounding trees. All these images come through the sense of sight. You do not resist or cling to any of these sights. So, as soon as seeing happens, all impressions it created in the system are immediately released. It gets recorded in the memory only as an overview which can be later recalled without any emotional tinge. The finer details would also not be available. This is a condition in which the incoming energy is said to have been freely processed. If all situations could be witnessed the way things outside the car window are seen, life would be free from suffering. Every sight would remain simple seeing – something that does not disturb us in any way. This is called living in the present. This means that life situations are seen as simple experiences which can touch the mind (may be the heart as well), without leaving any imprints. Does it mean that we should look at a violent ex-husband or a bad mouthed boss or someone who betrayed with absolute indifference and not allow our-self to feel anything? The answer is a categorical no. Not getting affected by the presence of these people only means that we refuse to let them take charge of our life. It does not mean that you stop taking action necessary to deal with them. After all, do you stop steering the car because you are not affected by the sights which speed past the car window?

Unfortunately, in actual life we live differently. We judge people and also keep notes of the same. We commonly make observations like "He looked at me indifferently" or "His affection was a put on." or "He was friendly and warm." People can be offended if they are looked through or looked at too minutely. To cope with these situations, they push the unpleasant feeling away. On the other hand in case of a pleasant occurrence, they try to hold it for a longer time. It is this tendency to either resist or cling which does not let the energy of the incident pass through our system. It now gets stuck within, and is called an 'impression' which is a psychological mark whose depth depends on the intensity with which it was obstructed or seized. This is quite unlike what happens to the energy of the things seen while driving – they go through smoothly without being pushed or pulled.

The following pictorial depiction explains what happens in heart centre when we receive stimulus and created.

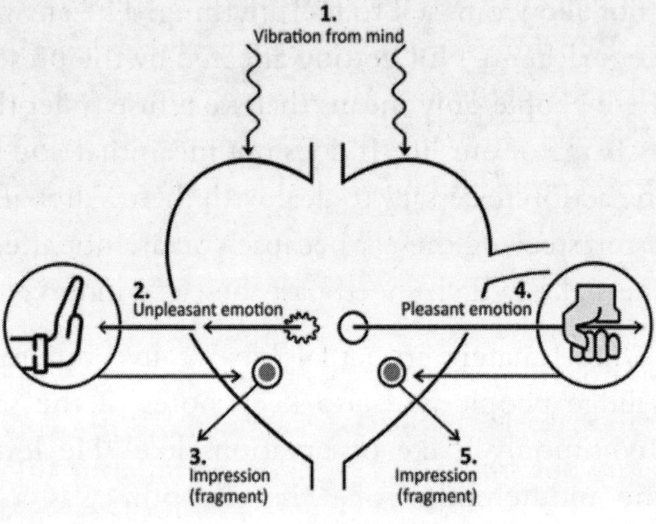


Figure-1

Diagram of heart centre

1. The mind generates vibrations on receiving stimulus through sense organs.
2. On receiving these vibrations if the heart generates unpleasant emotion, you will resist it.
3. The resistance mentioned in point 2 will create an impression (fragment).
4. On receiving these vibrations if the heart generates pleasant emotion, you cling to it.
5. The clinging at point 4 above will create an impression (fragment).

The working of a camera also explains this process well. A beautiful girl moves past the lens. The camera captures the photograph just the way she is, without modifying it in any way. And that is the end of the story. But things are different when the same image is formed in the eye of a young man. The image is recorded in memory, as it happened in case of the camera. If he clings to the energy (sight of the girl), it will not pass through. She will now occupy a large mind space. This marks the beginning of a love story. The young man starts planning ways of approaching her and imagines how it would be like to date her. Initially it was a simple sight of the girl but clinging begins to affect him in ways never experienced before. He can be carried away by a storm of thoughts and emotional upsurges – unlike the camera. Such men invite comments like: 'love is blind.' or 'love knows no bound.' or 'He is mad in love.' We are not suggesting that young men should refrain from seeking a fulfilling relationship and remain inert like a camera. To be like a camera, simply means not to get swept away by any emotional storm by staying tethered to the present.

Any energy, which fails to pass through, will first try to find release through thoughts. In the above case the mind of the young man may;

1. Chatter - I don't deserve her.

2. Make suggestions - May be this is not the right time to approach her.

3. Weave stories - Her family might not accept me.

4. Analysis - Did I leave a good impression on her?

5. Find rational solutions - It will be easier to meet her more frequently if I hired an apartment close to her home.

This activity of the mind does not help the energy to pass. So, after a while the trapped energy will seek release through emotional reactions. The man may become excited or happy if he finds a way to get through. But if she refuses to respond, he might get angry, depressed or ashamed. In our daily lives whenever the rising of an emotion is unpleasant, we instinctively avoid it; if it is pleasant, we instinctively hold it. In either case whether shoving it aside or grasping it tightly the energy of the stimulus gets stuck. This is how an impression, that we mentioned above, is formed. Every impression contains all details of thoughts, feelings and images related to an event. As a snapshot, it contains very minute details and can remain stored within for decades. That is why when an 'impression' formed by a childhood abuse comes to the surface years later, the associated fear and insecurity can also returns. People can remember their first date (sometimes, even after separating from their partner), with great relish. The euphoria of winning a race at the Olympics, or a keenly contested election is relived all through life. This happens because there is a corresponding "impression" which is getting stimulated.

In daily life the information stored in an impression does not keep popping up in the mind all the time. A person would become insane if that happens. Imagine an infinite number of impressions releasing memory and feelings of all the events that created them. It would blow your mind and heart apart. Human life would become unbearable. But this does not happen. It appears that nature builds a protective shield around the impression so that its contents do not easily pop up. An impression with shield around is called fragment. It can be imagined as capsules in which detailed information of an incident is stored. With the passage of time these fragments grow in numbers reducing the space available for flow of energy inside. It may be compared to calcium deposits that blocks the water pipes and fittings that reduces the flow of water. When fragments cause congestion in the path of energy, the heart is said to have closed to the extent of this clogging. In poetic language, it is called a broken heart. Nature made fragments to avoid continuous pain. But now they give rise to a permanent problem. More the clogging, lesser is the energy flow. Experientially, it means lesser joy. Things start appearing dark and depressing. Life becomes a burden. By habitually clinging or resisting sensations, we add to the existing stock of impressions on daily basis absolutely unaware that our inability to let things pass has serious ramifications. They are the seeds of suffering that we sow each day.

Although the fragments are stored in the heart, they remain closely connected with the mind as well. That is why when a particular event is recalled from the memory rack, the related fragment begins to open up. That is how the finer details of the event, including the feelings, begin to surface in awareness.

The following diagrams show the energy flow in the heart centre and the impact of clogging by fragments (shown as small circles) on the quality of our life.

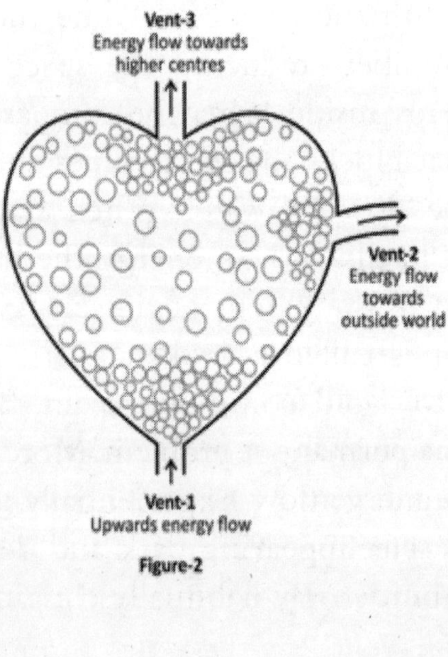


Figure-2

In the heart shown in figure 2, all the three vents are badly clogged. There is no passage available for the energy to flow upward. This is the heart of a sad, depressed person. No energy means no enthusiasm for life.

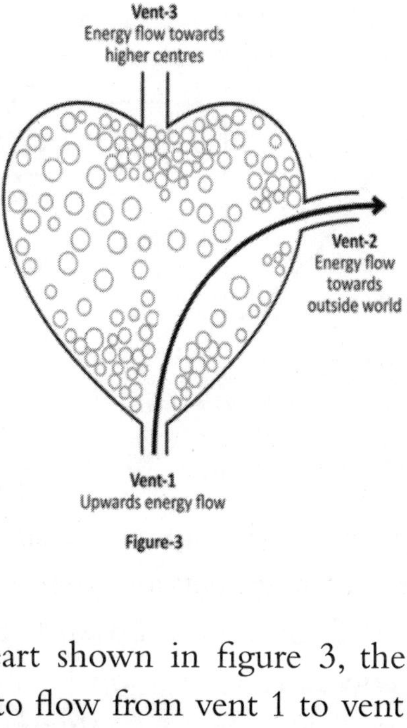

Figure-3

In the heart shown in figure 3, the energy has found a path to flow from vent 1 to vent 2. This state is usually achieved when we meet a loved one. This can also happen when a strong wish is granted. The vibrations received from the mind somehow moves the fragments in such a way that energy finds a way up and flows out of vent 2 towards the world outside. This flow brings a feeling of love and joy. If the current is strong enough, people outside will also feel this love and affection. Vent 2 is the point through which the energy gets connected with the outside world. When good things happen in life, it is the energy flowing through this vent that makes us feel happy.

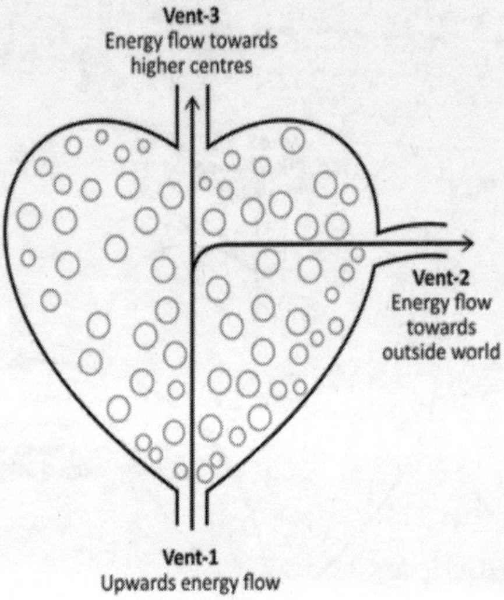


Figure-4

The heart shown in figure 4 is sufficiently open. There are very few fragments and energy flows through all three vents; from vent-1 upwards to vent-2 and vent-3. The consequent emotional state will be that of unconditional love for everything and everyone. A deep sense of awe and gratitude will fill you up with joy. You will be light hearted, elevated and rise above all worldly pettiness. People will be attracted towards you and feel warm comfort in your presence. The divine manifest in you.

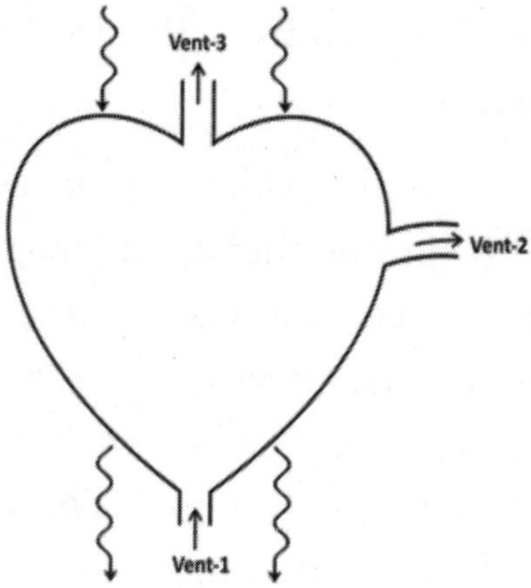


Figure-5

The heart shown in figure 5 is absolutely free from fragments. This state is achieved because all vibrations from the mind pass through without any resistance or clinging. It is possible only when there are no personal preferences, likes or dislikes. One has to be open and receptive to everything and everyone. This is heart in its purest form – the heart of a child.

The reason behind our joyful childhood is now easy to understand. A child has no preferences, so he does not resist or cling to an experience. As a result, energy of all stimuli pass through without creating impressions. Thus, there is no possibility of a child's heart ever getting clogged. He is a living camera. The free flow of energy manifests as bubbling joy which touches everyone deeply. But accumulation of blockages start as soon as the child develops a sense of identity – which is primarily made of likes and dislikes, expectations, preferences and prejudices. The consequence is disastrous – the joy of childhood is, sadly, lost forever.

There is enough medical evidence to show that many ailments of the heart, respiratory organs and immune system have their roots in the mind. In the field of mental health the correlation is direct. For example people who keep worrying become neurotic and those carrying guilt may get depressed. The way we respond or react to different events impacts our biological system thereby affecting physical health. All of us have very personal aversions and preferences which determines the extent to which we either resist or cling to experiences. If this tendency is high, fragments will be easily created causing severe clogging of the heart. Therefore, closing of the heart is a function of our psyche. If we can learn to let go, the spawning of fragments will be considerably reduced if not completely stop. The susceptibility of the heart to close will correspondingly reduce leading to considerable improvement in our physical and mental health.

In the context of opening and closing of the heart discussed above, few pertinent questions arise:

i. How is a thought or an emotion created?

ii. How does the mind store and retrieve an event?

iii. How does a thought stir a particular emotion?

iv. How are heart and mind connected?

v. How does energy flow?

Resisting or clinging to an experience, energy failing to pass through, formation of an impression, creation of a fragment, blocking of the heart and changes in energy flow are unfamiliar phrases to most people. Some may even demand evidence supported by laboratory research to establish their veracity. In fact the list of such questions can be endless. These questions are not important because the need to explain a phenomenon in terms of physical laws arise only in scientific research conducted in physical laboratories. Our approach here is experiential and not intellectual. It is enough if we can understand our real time experiences in terms of this vocabulary and can also make predictive analysis. The reader should be able to examine the truth of the assertions made in this chapter through the strength of his personal experiences without the need of any external support or equipment. The body-mind complex is a living laboratory, where experiments can be conducted, observations made and inferences drawn. The science of joyful living therefore becomes a study of the principles governing movement of and interrelation between thoughts, emotions and energy. It helps us to understand the body-mind complex on the basis of daily experiences, without recourse to biological or psychological concepts and terminologies.

To sum up, in an otherwise healthy body the other three constituents of the 'space within' are governed by the following six cardinal rules:

1. *Thoughts and emotions cannot be controlled; they disperse if allowed to freely float.*
2. *Feelings can get tagged to a particular thought.*
3. *If we resist or cling to a stimulus, its energy will not pass through.*
4. *The energy which does not pass through will create a psychic scar called 'impression' which contains all details of the event.*
5. *All impressions become fragments which cause blockages in the energy path.*
6. *The experience of joy diminishes when these fragments block energy path.*

These rules are new to us. We have no idea of their power to steer us towards joyful living. These are the rules of the game we play in pursuit of happiness. Is it not strange that we aspire to win this game without knowing the rules governing it? The consequences of this ignorance are not difficult to imagine.

---

We have used the words 'awareness' and 'psyche' repeatedly, without describing what they mean. Actually, they are two intrinsic attributes of the inner space that we will discuss in chapter 3.

# THE SPACE WITHIN

## Part Two

# Chapter 3

# THE SPACE WITHIN

## Part Two

The long evolutionary process endowed our body with a complex physiological structure and a strong instinct of survival. The unique psychological frame of each individual, which determines the way his thoughts and emotions move, is equally intricate. This psychosomatic entity called human being uses energy in multiple forms and ways. We have discussed the constituent elements of the 'space within' in the last chapter and also learnt the six cardinal rules governing them. But the nature of this 'inner space' and its power to make the experience of life possible comes from certain attributes that are inherent to it. These attributes influence the way our thoughts, emotions and energy function and therefore give rise to the possibility of steering them in a direction that makes our lives a pleasant experience.

These attributes are:

### 1. Awareness

Awareness is a field in which all our experiences arise. Anything which remains out of it, does not exist for us. The universe is perceived only in the way and to the extent that we are aware of it. For example, a snake under the bed is as good as not being there until it is discovered. In deep sleep, we are not aware of anything including our body and our mind. Without delving in popular theories offering scientific explanations of its reality, it is enough to acknowledge that awareness is a matter of everyday experience. We can become more aware of one thing and less of another. Arjuna, the great archer in Indian mythology, was asked by Dronacharya to target the eye of the bird. As Arjuna set the arrow and pulled the string, the Guru asked him to describe everything that was visible to him. "I see nothing but the eye." said Arjuna. For him the branches, leaves, sky and feathers did not exist. Similarly there are times when you are so absorbed in watching TV that you don't see a friend enter the room. This is in contrast to what happens while driving. You see people on sidewalks, the trees on both sides of the road, houses, shops, other cars on road at a glance. There is no focus on a particular object. Clearly, awareness works both like a spotlight (as in the case of Arjuna) and a floodlight (as in the case of driving) depending on the need.

The fact that awareness can engage intently with a particular object to the exclusion of other surrounding objects has serious implications. For example, while listening to music, awareness may shift to the sudden barking of a dog in the street or to the memory flash of your sick mother. In those few moments in which attention shifted, you could not listen to either the music or the lyric. The song had continued to play, but you were not there to hear it – you had gone to meet the dog. Clearly, awareness can be hijacked by an object even without our explicit effort.

Any external event, whether a sound or a sight or a mix of these, passes through the sense organs (the ears and the eyes in this case), producing auditory and visual sensation. By definition, any such sensation is an object in the inner space and awareness will get drawn towards it. Sense organs create an infinite number of such objects and our consciousness is continuously drawn into them. These objects could be anything – a desire, an insult or the memory of a marital conflict. The extent to which the awareness is drawn will depend on the nature of the individual i.e. his psyche. When this identification is total, the awareness will perceive itself as that object. For example, awareness can get fully sucked into grief, nervousness or fear. When this happens, a crushing emotional tsunami occurs, which leaves one shattered and exhausted. In this state, the person is said to have 'drowned in grief' or 'filled with fear'.

Imagine the death of a dear one. In the grand cosmic scheme it is just an event happening in one corner of the creation. But when it draws in your awareness, the grief amplifies so much so that it appears to be the only event that has happened in the universe. In fact, the power of sorrow becomes devastating when one gets completely identified with it. But if you are mindful enough so as not to let awareness be pulled in by a tragic event, its psychological impact will be considerably reduced. It is like grabbing the rescue ropes to pull oneself out of an emotional storm. But since most of us are not mindful enough therefore we cannot see these ropes let alone use them. It needs a lot of training before the skill necessary to harness them is acquired.

It is important to recognize the unchanging nature of awareness. We establish our identity using religion, family, status, education and many such descriptions. But these characteristics are not permanent in nature. Similarly, things like health, mood, relationships and understanding also change. If everything that we use to describe ourselves is subject to change, the question is do you change with them? This is a complex question to ask. To answer it, we must define "You." let's find the answer by examining our response to the following questions:

1. When you were ten years old and looked into the mirror did you see a ten year old body?

2. Now when you are twenty-five do you see the same child or an adult?

The answer is clear. Earlier you saw a child, and later you see an adult. Obviously what was being looked at in the mirror (i.e. what was reflected by the mirror) changed. But what about the one who was actually looking or was trying to note if there was a difference? Did he also change? Don't hurry as you contemplate on this very important query. Look for your own answer. If possible, discuss this with a close friend.

Take it a little further. You see dreams while sleeping; who is it that is actually dreaming? You reply "I see the dreams." And if you are looking out of the window to see the distant mountains, who is seeing the mountains? You will again say, "It's me". Now, you know that this I/me, who saw the dream and also the mountains, did not change on both occasions. There is a continuity of something which is not amenable to change – something that we can call the continuity of the being. This is the unchanging nature of this inner space.

Suppose someone shows you a photograph of an unknown man and asks, "Is that you?" Your answer will be "No". The reply is easy, because the object is clearly separate and identifiable. This is the simplest form of subject-object relationship. If we look at the feelings, thoughts and also the chattering partner closely, they are no different from any object like the photograph mentioned above. You experience them; therefore they are as separate from you as any object in the room is. They can at best be called objects of the inner world, and you continue to be the subject. Many people find it difficult to recognize their thoughts or emotions as separate objects. It happens because their attention is completely absorbed in these so called inner objects. In this condition, subject and object both merge, i.e. they become one at the level of consciousness. Now there would be no possibility of you existing separately. In other words, the partner pulls in our awareness to such an extent that we start identifying ourselves with him.

Whether we can perceive it or not, the fact remains that there is a subject-object relationship between you and your thoughts (and emotions). This is so because everything is just an appearance in the awareness. Awareness knows that a particular object exists and also knows that it knows. This attribute helps in creating a distance between our self and an object of inner space, say a thought or an emotion. Because of this gap, the object can be watched from a distance like gazing at clouds in the sky. In this state of being, the object fails to draw in awareness and therefore does not affect us. This ability to watch is a powerful tool of transformation. People tide over the tsunamis of inner turbulence when they manage to create a gap between themselves and the disturbance. They begin to see the most overwhelming situation as an appearance which gradually fades away without blowing them away. It is like sitting on the bank of a river watching the stream flow past.

## 2. The Will

Awareness is not something that cannot be manipulated. We have already mentioned that there is an innate capacity to bring it to focus on selected objects. As discussed earlier, it can be used both as a spotlight and a floodlight. This ability is made possible by virtue of another attribute of the inner space called the Will. It makes awareness move in the desired direction. The body, thoughts, emotions and energy together do not create a helpless being destined to be tossed around. When you wish to move in a particular direction, it's the Will that commands; the brain, nervous system and muscles follow its diktat. You want to focus attention on a mathematical equation; it is the Will that commands the mind to do so. It is a strong force which helps in making and carrying a resolve through to the desired end. In many meditative practices, disciples are instructed to shift their attention from one point on the body to another, say from left shoulder to the naval. This is made possible only by the use of Will. This powerful attribute is a valuable gift of nature; one that gives us an opportunity to master the inner world.

Any question about the source of Will and whether free Will really exists is not relevant to our discussion here. It is enough to acknowledge the fact that we use it everyday and also experience its close relationship with awareness.

## 3. The Psyche

As stated earlier, we can move awareness in the desired direction. This 'desire' arises from a complex structure called 'Psyche' which is another attribute of the inner space. The Psyche is responsible for processing the stimuli (received through the senses), storing it with or without modifications, and retrieving it at the appropriate moment. Again, it is not important to know the exact science of this process. It is enough to admit that it is a matter of daily experience. The yelling of the boss or a childhood abuse is rarely forgotten. The sight of the setting sun or a first romance or the aroma of an Indian curry can be nostalgic. Psyche determines whether love, hate, shame, discontentment, fear or some other emotion will be stoked in a given situation. Perhaps no reader would dispute that all this data is stored within. It is also a matter of experience that storing a stimulus is not a passive process. It is a dynamic exercise because the incoming information combines methodically with the relevant data already stored. This mixing depends on the unique thought process which the individual possess. The partner scripts and narrates his own version of what happened. Therefore, both the form and substance of what finally gets registered in the memory can be very different from what was initially received.

As an illustration, let us take the situation of a woman who meets her ex-husband by a sudden chance. This meeting begins when the image of the man, on the street outside, is projected on her mind-screen. The partner immediately remarks, "Oh! The shameless rascal." This takes a split second only. The memory rack identified him as the ex-husband and the partner loses no time in making the remark. This narration depends much upon the kind of thoughts the woman had stored earlier within. The images of the first incident of marital violence, which happened years ago, can suddenly surface. On another occasion, instead of the discord, she might recall her first candlelight dinner together after marriage. In real terms, the woman has only seen a man. But there is a whole 'complex arrangement' of thought patterns, memories, emotional surges and past experiences that get together to create a totally new drama within. This "complex arrangement" is called the psyche. The psyche is like a computer software that runs the mind, depending on earlier experiences, including all our prejudices, judgments, views and ideas. Since it is unique to an individual, every person responds differently to the same event.

*There is a Zen story of a Buddhist monk who lived in a monastery. One day, the Master finds him very vibrant and effused with light. "What happened?" he asks the disciple. The monk replied "There is big Oak tree in the courtyard that I see every day. For the first time today I saw just the tree. It was only the pure sight of the tree and nothing else. The tree did not stimulate any thought patterns from the past. It took me beyond myself." It was a pure experience of seeing a simple tree, which awakened the monk. In that moment, the psyche did not come between him and the tree.*

This story underlines the fact that mind does not allow us to see things as they are. A stimulus is experienced only after it is colored by the existing patterns of thinking stored inside us. It needs some practice to watch how subtle and seemingly innocuous the tricks of the mind can be. It can modify anything that is taken in for processing. The mind is like a veil through which we see the outside world. The moment it is lifted, the experience of 'just tree' will arise. It is important to know that the stored patterns are not necessarily undesirable. Actually they help us to live harmoniously in a civilized society. After all we have to fulfill expectations, comply with norms of dignified behavior and present ourselves as predictable members of society. It is possible only if we create patterns within and follow them in our everyday lives. The issue, however, is to recognize that when we live an unexamined life they come in the way of unconditional joy.

Even though medical science has understood human body in great depth, yet psyche i.e. the manner in which sensory inputs are received, stored, retrieved and processed, continues to baffle. Scientific attempts to understand it is, at best, work in progress.

These three attributes of the inner space, along with six cardinal rules mentioned in chapter 2, together determine the whole matrix of our life. They influence the way we perceive the outside world. When this perception is positive, the world is a pleasant place to be in. Otherwise, it can feel like hell.

# THE FOUR NAVIGATORS

## Chapter 4

# The Four Navigators

Life experiences swing between the pleasant and the unpleasant depending on whether our wants are fulfilled or not. When things go wrong, life becomes a burden. However, when the desired results are achieved we feel good. There appears to be a direct relationship between our happiness and fulfillment of desires. This means that the outside world is determining the way we experience life. Very often we miss how intricately everything in and around us is interconnected with the rest of the universe. In that sense we are inter-beings i.e. dependent for our existence on rest of the cosmos. This inter-dependence implies that at any point in time, we cannot be in absolute control of anything. Our wishes and efforts are not the exclusive factors that determine whether a particular thing will happen or not. So, anyone who thinks that happy life is made possible only by the fulfillment of our wishes is in for disappointment. Happiness is a matter of the world inside; it shall always remain elusive if you will search it in the world outside.

People suggest activities which make life happier and satisfying. Some of them are:

1. Helping: Doing things for others
2. Giving: Sharing with others
3. Relating: Connecting with people
4. Exercising: Taking care of your body
5. Trying Out: Keep learning new things
6. Directing: Having goals to look forward to
7. Thanking: Being grateful to others
8. Involving: Being part of something bigger

These activities, if assimilated in our daily routine, make life an enriching experience. That sounds simple but we all know how difficult it is to continue performing them over a long span of time. Some activities like exercising and helping are simple. Others like thanking need serious reflection in order to understand how profound they can be.

In any action-based approach, we have to keep an account of things done. There will always be slip-ups which need timely correction. This is an onerous task, not easy to sustain. It is common to see how new year resolutions and the enthusiasm that accompanies them fizzles out in no time. The "Actions for Happiness", usually start with great fanfare and meet the same fate. People start with one activity. Very often, repetition of an activity runs the risk of becoming mechanical and boring especially when the expected results are not forthcoming. Also each of these activities demand engagement with other people. So there is an inherent dependence on the outside world. This is a very inefficient way of trying to live joyfully. There is no denying that the approach of 'doing things for happiness' can bring a sense of satisfaction and fulfillment. Many people devote a lot of time and energy in making this a kind of mission in their lives. All these activities certainly serve a useful purpose at both personal and social level. But to seek lasting happiness we must dive deep to reach the spring of joy within us.

Ideally, any approach to joyous life should be comprehensive. It should be both easy to understand and apply. Therefore a single prescription in place of a long list of "Actions for Happiness" would be easy to remember and practice. It should be more of mind training and less of an activity in the traditional sense. More so, it must work in good, bad and the ugly life-conditions. Earlier in this book we learnt how letting the energy of an event pass through is the key to living in the highest possible order. It keeps the heart unclogged and the consequent free flow of energy keeps us in a joyful state. In that context, the simplest prescription is:

*"Keep your heart open."*

This is a mantra not meant to be verbalized but understood and lived every moment. Reading or memorizing it a thousand times over will not bring any transformative experience. It has to become a part of our very being – like our heartbeat and breath. The question now is – how can we keep the heart open in the humdrum of daily life?

The answer is:

1. Live in **G**ratitude
2. Live **R**esponsibly
3. Live in **A**cceptance
4. Live to **F**orgive

Living in four different ways sounds complex. They appear as four distinct categories to almost everyone. However, in practice they are not. Each way of living carries within its fold the quintessence of the other three. So at a deeper level they are essentially one. You cannot live in a particular way in total exclusion of other three. Living in one, will actually be akin to living in all four. In chapter 9, the truth of this assertion will become self evident. The capacity of Gratitude,

Responsibility, Acceptance and Forgiveness (we shall henceforth use the acronym **GRAF** to address them collectively) to steer human life away from suffering is not easy to recognize. The eco-system in which we are brought up does not foster these traits. Our mind is not trained to be naturally grateful, responsible, accepting and forgiving. Moreover there are enough 'vendors of happiness' around who easily influence gullible majority onto the paths that promise joy but actually lead to unmitigated sorrow.

The four constituents of GRAF are in fact four 'navigators'. The nomenclature 'navigator' comes from their power in "Making You Turn" in a direction that leads to a joyful life. As a navigational tool GRAF operates on scientific principles and its efficacy can be tested through personal experience. There is no dogma, ritual, worshipping or praying involved. Gratitude, responsibility, acceptance and forgiveness are basically qualities, which if imbibed and assimilated, keep the flow of energy through heart unrestricted. Such open heart is the mother of unconditional happiness. Unconditional because this happiness does not depend on other people, events or situations – more specifically the world around.

We will learn in the following chapters that a person with genuinely grateful or responsible disposition is not vulnerable to new blockages. Those who are responsible effectively allow all kinds of disturbing energies to pass through without forming blockages. Acceptance allows 'What is' to be clearly seen so that we can find our correct location on the map of life, enabling us to choose the right direction while exploring the space within. Forgiveness is a powerful remedy for dissolving old fragments. The navigational strength of GRAF essentially comes from its power to dissolve blockages and stop spawning of new ones. This requires deep commitment and regular practice of simple techniques designed to raise awareness. Reading and appreciating the way GRAF works cannot make you experience its power to transform. It has to be lived each day, nay each moment. And "living it" means that you:

i) Understand what GRAF means; and

ii) Practice GRAF in everyday life situations with unwavering conviction.

So it is a two step process. The first is to know what it means. The second is to devote oneself to this knowing – a devotion that is absolute and unshakeable. But this is not easy to happen. Your upbringing, lifestyle, beliefs, ideas of happiness and a deep sense of identity stands in the way. Only the courageous and determined ones can live in **G**ratitude, **R**esponsibility, **A**cceptance and **F**orgiveness.

Are you one of them?

# G FOR GRATITUDE

Chapter 5

# G For Gratitude

Many people feel that they do not have enough good things in their life. They find their wealth, social prestige, relationships and achievements inadequate. No amount of possessions and accomplishments, physical or abstract, satisfies them. Their relentless yearning for 'more' never brings 'enough'. For most of us successful pursuit of our desires is the highest achievable gratification. Somehow, all the worldly gains put together do not give anyone lasting happiness. It is understandable to find a poor man craving for money. But how do we explain the insatiable hunger for riches of the wealthy? The answer is simple – the rich feel as much 'inadequacy' as the poor and with the same intensity. They focus unwaveringly on wants which turns them blind to the riches already possessed. Such feeling of deficiency can fade away not by acquisition of additional goodies, but by shifting attention to the abundance that life offers in each moment.

But people do not readily accept the viewpoint that there are enough good things in their lives at any point in time. The reason is simple – on one side they lack the ability to see the existing plenty and on the other they are good at keeping count of things which could not be acquired. If you point out to good things already available, they will view it as an attempt to pacify them. "Oh! You have no idea about how difficult my life is. Nothing good has ever happened to me." they may cry out. Almost everyone believes that the approach to see abundance will destroy competitive spirit. It is argued that if there are already enough goodies, why would men work towards acquiring more. It will breed complacency making it impossible to build a progressive society. For most people, the idea of having plentiful is a ploy meant to keep them content with their existing state of affair so that they do not create unrest in the community.

Any claim about having 'plenty' in life should be carefully investigated. We must arrive at an evidence-based conclusion to ascertain if this claim is indeed a fact or is merely fiction. If it is indeed true, one should be able to write at least fifty wonderful things that happened today. People, who do not live an examined life, will jump at this expectation. "Fifty! Are you crazy? Maybe I can write one or two at the most" they may say.

Let us look at few things that happened in last 24 hours:

1. Waking up in the morning
2. Breathing normally
3. Hearing
4. Seeing
5. Tasting
6. Smelling
7. Water in the shower
8. Air-conditioning
9. Drinking a cup of tea
10. Sitting in a chair
11. Return of children from school
12. Reaching office
13. A functioning toilet

These are routine things happening every day and by itself do not prove any point. However, the importance of this list will become clear if we look at it from a different viewpoint. For example, more than fifty thousand people all over the world die every night and many more struggle to recover from disabling medical conditions. What makes you so confident that you would wake up in the morning tomorrow? Is it not a cause for celebration that, so far, you have not been one of them. Are we not missing this important fact by considering getting up in the morning as trite? Look at item 12 on this list – return of children from school. Now imagine that one evening they do not return. What would your predicament be? How would you feel then? Pause and think...

Please read each entry in the list above once again. Take a pause and imagine none of these happen. Do you still think they are mundane, unimportant events that do not add up to the stock of what is good in life? Try visualizing the consequences when what we dismiss as routine does not happen. Feel the frustration when the toilet does not flush; you are unable to breath or sit in a chair comfortably. You will realize that these seemingly trivial occurrences are actually blessings. In fact, a large number of people think you are endowed with a rich life and they earnestly wish to live the same.

The reason for the inability to identify the good things is simple – we do not have the capacity to identify them. We take too many things for granted. Every day events, which go unnoticed, become acutely important only when the routine is breached – like children not returning home from school in the evening. Now, make a list of things that happen every day that you take for granted. Take each item one by one and imagine it will not happen today.

Suddenly you will realize how much existing good is being routinely ignored. We habitually forget our good health, material comforts, affection of family or a help received. Instead we spend a lot of our time thinking about things that we wish should happen or should not happen. In terms of neurology, neural firing flows and neural connections grow in the direction in which our attention goes. So, if the attention repeatedly goes towards scarcity you will begin to permanently feel a sense of lacking and inadequacy. But if with practice we can move attention towards abundance a new default neuron network will be created in the brain. The universe will now appear to be a kind and generous giver. The abundance becomes visible. We are a far richer generation than our ancestors; we routinely live longer than our grandparents and enjoy luxuries and personal freedom which they could never imagine. Is it not unfortunate that people still choose to focus on what they do not have?

Perhaps, you can easily write more than fifty things now.

## What is Gratitude?

Gratitude is not a verbal expression although it may find one. It is a feeling which swells up in the heart when you receive a gift unconditionally – similar to what is experienced in deep devotion or in the moment of loving emotion.

The path of gratitude is, in essence, the path of love. The echo of the biblical quotes: "thou shall love thy neighbor as thyself" and "let all that you do be done in love" can be heard in all other religions as well. It does not matter if the language and the expressions of their preaching is different. But such profound statements are nothing more than a string of pious words for the majority. People do not know ways of actualizing these preachings. They force themselves to practice love for the proverbial neighbor or make efforts to do things in love. This breeds hypocrisy instead. The love such people cherish or demonstrate is nothing but camouflaged desire or lust. But in case of those who live in gratitude, love happens. The litmus test of authentic love is as follows:

*If anything that you claim is 'love' but it makes a demand on the other person, then it is not love but a potential seed of hatred. But if anything makes you give unconditionally, then it can be nothing but love.*

You can now easily check the truth of any claim of love. Most of our relationships, which ostensibly are based on mutual love and affection, involve set of very subtle expectations. We want fidelity, care, affection, help in the times of need and much more from our loved ones. These are demands, and they take the relations through a roller coaster ride-sometimes high and many a times low. We are elated when our expectations are met but we stop loving (and may even start hating instead) if the hopes are belied.

Gratitude is a deep recognition that everything is received by virtue of universal grace and not on the basis of what we do or think we are entitled to. This dilutes the feeling of being the doer. The ego takes a backseat and a deep sense of oneness with everything around is felt. This makes the grateful man loving. He does not make an effort to love anyone – he personifies it.

The real stock-keeping of our endowments is not possible unless life is seen from a position of gratitude. If existing good is recognized and appreciated first, the suffering arising out of the sense of inadequacy will begin to fade. Gratitude arises when you

i. Recognize having received a particular thing

ii. Treat it as a gift, and

iii. Appreciate it in the heart (at emotional and not intellectual level)

The word 'gift' is important. If you believe it has been earned by the sweat of brow or strength of the arm, gratitude will not arise. The role of existence in our achievements cannot be seen if "I did it" is the dominant feeling. You have to recognize a fundamental fact that "what is now and here" exists by virtue of a combination of innumerable factors at play in the Universe – most of them are beyond our control. That is why the wise say, "things do not happen by the force of your merit but through the compassion and grace of nature".

Those who subscribe to the merit of living in gratitude often say:

- The Universe is a generous giver;
- Gratitude increasingly attracts abundance, and
- This power to bring more should make us even more grateful

To a rational thinker these affirmations are in the nature of hypothesis whose truth must be ascertained. This is possible only experientially and not scientifically. Anyone wanting to confirm these affirmations must start with preparing his list of 'fifty things' as 'proof of plenty'. If the heart does not fill up with gratitude, the truth will never be known first hand. It is essential to step into the pool to know how it feels to be in water. No amount of reading or writing can give us that experience. The list of plenty will become longer only if the practice succeeds in cultivating gratitude. Jesus Christ said "Whosoever hath, to him more shall be given, and he shall have abundance, but whosoever hath not, from him shall be taken away even that he hath". It would be easier to understand if it is rephrased as "Whosoever hath **gratitude**, to him more shall be given, and he shall have abundance, but whosoever hath not **gratitude**, from him shall be taken away even that he hath." This simply means that abundance will manifest when we live in gratitude. Our capacity to see is enhanced. It was always there but we did not have the eye to perceive it.

We reach out to support and sympathize with people when a tragedy strikes them. In those moments, the uncertainty of life and possibility of permanent loss occurring suddenly appear real. Rendering help to a family in distress is important. But such circumstances can bring about transformation if we ask "Could it have happened to me?" But people avoid such question. It is a taboo to indulge in such unpleasant thoughts. When you see failure, death, sickness and injustice afflict others, remember you are equally vulnerable to them. Be grateful if you have been spared so far. When perceived in this light, such incidents make us realize and appreciate the presence of things which are going right in life. Anyone who genuinely understands this will find that his "list of plenty" is always incomplete. For such a person gratitude is not the outcome of a new good thing coming in life. Instead, it is the result of the recognition that things did not go wrong despite innumerable ways in which they could have.

The article "Bless it all" written by Julie Keene illustrates that it is possible for some people to see good even in the most trying life situations. She writes:

*"My oldest son Richard died when he was nine. I am so very grateful that I know that each soul uses its*

*earth school experiences including the manner and time of departure from the Earth plane. My second son Robert nearly died when he was two and suffered brain damage as a result of the illness. I am grateful that I know that Robert chose this earth school lesson and as his mother I chose the experience with him. I have felt much pain watching him struggling with life but he has demanded from me, and thus has taught me, unconditional love. Such a great gift."*

Her comments may not sound credible to many. How can anyone say all this in a life situation like the one Julie was in? This is possible only when acceptance of things happening to us is absolute. Then all inner conflicts come to rest and peace is restored in mind. This enables one to view even worst of a condition positively and to be thankful for whatever good is seen. Some people see only thorns in a rose bush; whereas others admire the rose amidst thorns. Intellectually, both statements may seem equivalent, but at emotional level they are not. Thorns in a rose bush is a complaint – an expression of resentment. But to see and appreciate a rose amidst thorns is being grateful to nature. These two different views about the same thing creates a corresponding unique internal chemical state affecting our health, sense of empowerment and joy in its own distinct way. The gratitude in Julie does not allow any kind of asking – there is no precondition. The Universe is free to bestow anything and at any time.

## Benefits of Gratitude

In good times, people take their circumstances for granted. They forget their innate vulnerability. But misfortunes make it clear that we are powerless in the face of unpredictability. Everything counted on for security can be snatched away in a moment, mostly without any warning. Although people seem to know this truth, yet they behave like eternal beings. A deep recognition of mortality can dilute the strong sense of entitlement that most people carry. The significance of many things we ordinarily ignore or consider trivial becomes obvious when their transitory nature is recognized. Recall thirteen routine items listed earlier in the chapter. How did you feel on imagining that children did not return from school in the evening? Such negative visualizations including thoughts like "I can be dead anytime" has enormous potential of transforming the way we live. It can make us say a thanks giving prayer without waiting for something good to happen. We begin to see abundance all around. This is the power of knowing that everything is impermanent.

There is an old saying "virtue is its own reward". Perhaps no other trait demonstrates the truth of this adage more than gratitude. Gratitude does not coexist with sorrow or resentment. It has capacity to enhance quality of life by energizing and transforming us in myriad ways. We become more helpful, outgoing, optimistic and trustworthy without any recourse to traditional moral lessons. Old hurts begin to heal and fear of future uncertainties diminishes. One moves from obsession to detachment, fear to love and scarcity to abundance. It becomes easier to stay peaceful and be mindfully present in the moment. Gratitude can fill you up with childlike awe as you begin to notice the care that the cosmic forces take to nurture existence. Scientific evidence suggests that grateful people are more resilient to stress. This happens because gratitude tethers the mind firmly to the present moment. The mind slows down and the chattering, which otherwise goes on endlessly, is considerably reduced. This improves immune function, develops a happier disposition and produces a sense of well-being. Doctors have reported that patients who are grateful for therapeutic sessions and appreciate the prescriptions progress well. But those who unnecessarily worry and suspect or believe that treatment should be less expensive do not show as good a recovery.

*A man sat begging by the roadside. A board placed nearby read*

*"I am blind. Please help me".*

*His begging bowl was almost empty. A man went up to him and asked*

*"Can I rewrite the board".*

*"Yes sure if that helps" said the beggar.*

*The man made some changes and went away. Within few hours the begging bowl was full. The beggar realized that something had really changed. Curious, he stopped the next man who came up to drop money into the bowl.*

*"Can you tell me what is written on the board, Sir" he asked.*

*The donor looked at the board and read aloud the words written on it "What a beautiful morning. Alas! I cannot see it".*

What is the difference between the two expressions? "I am blind. Please help me" is a statement of fact and also a cry for assistance. But by saying, "Alas! I cannot see it," the beggar is subtly conveying that "you can see". The second message brings home the blessing of eyesight. In daily routine you stop appreciating your ability to see till the blindness of another person shakes you up. The value of a natural gift, which was taken as a matter of fact, becomes obvious. This revelation makes people thankful which in turn inspire acts of kindness.

## Dimensions of gratitude

A grateful man gives without remembering and takes without forgetting. He feels obliged not only when he receives a gift but also when someone accepts his offering. In Indian culture it is common to make an additional donation while giving alms. This is done out of a sense of gratitude to the person for accepting the alms. This is authentic humility in its full glory.

'Being grateful' and a 'grateful being' are two different things. The first is a behavioral trait and transactional in nature. It happens in everyday life when we thank others for rendering help or giving a gift. The second is a state of being – a manifestation of 'authentic humility' mentioned above. A grateful being cannot be an exhibitionist; he cannot display humility as a conscious effort. It is not a practice or a discipline for him, but an understanding. Anyone making efforts to be humble means that he is treating humility as a kind of personal goal to be achieved. Remember anything you think has been achieved is never seen as a gift. It will not let you be truly humble or grateful. A grateful being does not consider that he is the doer and achiever. He believes that things happen by virtue of universal grace. This recognition waters down the ego and suddenly we begin to see the universe as a generous giver.

The phrase "thank you" has unfortunately become a salutation – a mechanical response to things received. It is also used as a civilized way to end an interpersonal communication much like saying hello. A child thinks that 'thanks giving' is a social obligation when he is prodded by mother to say "thank you uncle" for the birthday gift. The difference between verbalizing and feeling thanks is never driven home. It is important to understand this fine distinction. The concept of thanks giving as ordinarily understood implies that thanks should be offered to someone because an occasion for it has arisen. It is recognition of having received a gift. This is "feeling grateful "which is event based. But "being grateful" is very different. It is a state of being in which there is no reason, like receiving a gift, for being grateful. You just revel in the existing plenty.

There are four dimensions of gratitude:

i. **Intensity:** Given a particular event, different people will feel different levels of gratitude. Intensity is an indicator of our disposition towards gratefulness.

ii. **Frequency:** Some people report that they feel little or no gratitude whereas others experience it several times over the same period. The number of times one feels grateful in a day is the frequency of gratitude.

iii. **Span:** Span of gratitude refers to the number of situations for which a person can feel grateful at any given time. Some people acknowledge their jobs, families, health and wealth as gifts of nature. Others think they have earned them. The gratitude span of the latter group is shorter.

iv. **Density:** For a given situation or an outcome, it refers to the number of persons to whom one feels grateful. If two persons who have won the same award are asked to make a list of people who contributed to their success, the number of people on these lists will be different. Those with higher density of gratitude will have a longer list, readily recognizing the contribution of parents, siblings, teachers, colleagues, superiors and even God.

## Gratitude and Evolution

Evolution did not endow human beings with a sense of gratitude, even though it is undoubtedly one of the most useful traits. Surely it is not a case of oversight by nature. To understand why this did not happen, it would be necessary to recapitulate the manner in which Homo sapiens emerged as the most dominant species in the biosphere. That will make the reasons obvious.

Evolution is inherently a slow process. It gave organisms and their ecosystem enough time to adjust to each other. If the lion became more adept at hunting, the deer became faster at running in the meantime. But in the case of humans, things happened differently. Their evolutionary rise was too fast and spectacular. From being ordinary nomadic forest hunter-gatherer, man formed settlements and communities. It did not take him long to start using mental faculties for dominating other species. The shift from the use of stone to iron and then copper had serious implications. This growth trajectory was too steep, making it impossible for other species to adapt themselves to the changes that humans had unleashed. In fact, human beings themselves found it difficult to adjust to their own fast changing state. As they began to exercise more power over other species, fear and anxieties grew. The urge to make future safer and more secure became stronger by the day. This required men to identify things that had gone wrong in the past and also to keep an eye on those likely go wrong in future. Probable threats had to be foreseen and timely action taken to remedy them. This thought process forced them to pay greater attention to things going wrong. There was no felt need to focus on things going right. As a consequence, the awareness was drawn towards existing and anticipated deficiencies. "What should be" became the dominant concern and "what is" took a backseat. This marked the beginning of the 'race for more'. A human mind conditioned to function in this mode cannot tune itself to the presence of abundance. It remained preoccupied with existing and imagined shortcomings. In such conditions, there was no space for gratitude to take root. Homo sapiens became successful in terms of physical survival on the strength of evolutionary process. However, the same process did not contribute anything in terms of making them joyful.

## Gratitude–Rights, Responsibilities and Efforts

The system of governance in ancient times was generally ruler-centric where the king was the final authority. There was no element of objective consideration, and subjective satisfaction of the ruling elite was enough to justify any action. Over time however, modern systems of administration emerged and gradually citizen became central to administrative arrangements. In recent times, a culture of constitutional or statutory rights has developed. Right to food, education, property, professing a particular religion, public services and justice is well-known. This system of governance has encouraged people to claim things as a matter of right – leaving no space for a sense of gratitude to grow. This is not to say that the sense of entitlement is a new phenomenon. There have always been men who thought they deserve to be treated as superior to others. By virtue of their influence they expect special treatment, including exemptions from applicable laws. They want others to behave in particular ways and resent it if that does not happen. The modern governance, based on rights approach, has increased their numbers manifold.

Family life offers another interesting illustration. There is usually an unsaid division of labour between spouses. In India the husband traditionally handled matters outside the household – a fulltime job, providing safety and comfort to family and determining social relationships. The wife looks after the children, their schooling and the kitchen. Even though this stereotype is not universally applicable any longer, still it applies to a large number of families. A job, assigned under this division of labour, is like performing a duty. In this situation, if the wife gives an account of her daily chores, the husband reacts, "So what? Aren't you supposed to do these tasks." So the household work is viewed as part of her responsibility matrix. Similarly, the wife thinks that the husband is fulfilling his set of duties by supporting the family. There is no obligation because every husband is expected to do so. But if both husband and wife learn to see the tasks done by each other as a gift to the family, a fundamental shift in perception will take place, which improves the quality of their relationship. This will make family life far happier than what it usually is.

Generally speaking, all of us believe that we achieve things by dint of hard work. Such claims are not totally false; after all we make efforts to get things done. But the point to ponder is this – can anyone honestly claim that things are owned or won or achieved only because of the personal efforts made? Was there nothing that came by way of contribution from other people, situations or events? By close observation, you can count many factors, most of them beyond our control, that influenced every outcome claimed as our achievement. It might appear that winning a medal in a race is your achievement. But is it really so? You could do it because of the support of the coach, parents, teachers and the spectators. Your food, transport, clothes, health, exercising equipment etc. were made possible due to the contribution of hundreds of people. Even your breath, which is essential before any attempt to run is made, is happening because of infinitely complex relation between the earth, sun, rain and the forests. Are any of these under your control in any way? If your existence depends on countless factors, can any accomplishment be attributed exclusively to your efforts? Stop here and ponder. This is a profound understanding which may help you to see the oneness that connects everything in the universe. This why Buddha said that we are inter-beings.

Now take a pause and do the following exercises:

1. Look around and notice things in the room. There is a chair, an air conditioner, a desktop, an electrical switchboard and many other items. Are you taking these things for granted? Most likely, yes. Do they add value to your life? Are you grateful to these material comforts? You may not be grateful to the computer but you can be grateful for it. We become so accustomed to the convenience of the appliances that make our lives comfortable that we never wonder what life would be without them.

2. Make a list of people who have helped you at some point in your life. Do you feel thankful for what they did for you? Have you ever expressed thanks to the sweeper who cleans the public roads or the farmer who grows vegetables you buy or the taxi driver who took you to the airport? If you have not done it, why?

We generally view the task performed by others, whether in a professional, familial or societal context, as a duty discharged or a responsibility fulfilled. The taxi driver, sweeper, waiter in restaurant, clerk in the office or the policeman on road are only doing an assigned job. We never feel thankful to them. We feel entitled to their services because they are paid for doing it. However, the attitude of gratitude enables us to perceive the tasks performed by them as a gift to us. Watch the sweeper cleaning the floor of your office or a waiter serving a cup of coffee or a mason plastering the wall of your house. Have you ever felt thankful to them? If not, why? Such thoughts do not occur to most of us – not even once in lifetime. Is this not a sorry state of affairs?

Many societies believe that children must abide by the wishes of their elders. When the son decides to marry a girl against the wishes of his parents, they very often make emotionally charged statements like "Is this the way you pay us back for what we did all for you in all these years?"They think that by disobeying the son is being ungrateful. This is keeping accounts in parent-child relation, which is otherwise so sacred. There is an obligation on children for having been brought-up and they must return it by fulfilling the expectations of their parents. Similarly many high sounding values like altruism, sense of duty, social conscience are inspired by this kind of score-keeping. We are told never to forget the contribution of our family, society and country in nurturing us. When the right time comes, we are expected to repay it. Young minds all over the world are inspired to cultivate this trait. Most of us consider this natural and inherently justified. After all what is wrong in making demands of paying back? People view relationships as assets in which time, energy and money is invested. It should not be surprising that they expect returns on it? Such transactional relations are useful in building a social system on the principle of mutual benefit but does not create an environment in which authentic humility can be nurtured. If people learn to be profoundly thankful, they would not need reminders about what others did for them. They would reciprocate not out of any sense of obligation but out of a deep sense of gratitude.

To sum up, the evolutionary process, socio-cultural ethos, formal education and value structure did not create an eco-system necessary to nurture gratitude. Therefore it is essential to make efforts to cultivate it. The flame of gratitude is low and small. It has to be protected from the winds of materialism, competitiveness, sense of entitlement and achievements. This is much more challenging than scaling mountains or swimming across turbulent seas.

## Tools for cultivating Gratitude

Gratitude is much more than mere verbal expression addressed to the person who gives us a gift. It is a way of life that does not need any give and take. It is a matter of knowing, feeling and living the mantra known as 'thank you'. For reasons discussed above, gratitude is not our default response. It does not come naturally like other emotions like love, jealousy, anger or regret. We need to constantly work to make gratitude a part of our being – like heart beat and breathing.

The following techniques help make it happen.

### 1. Journaling Gratitude

Writing down things has many advantages over plain thinking. It helps us to organize thoughts, improve integration and give context to things. Many psychological therapies emphasize on writing about all kinds of life experiences. They require people to write at least 100 pages about their emotions like resentments, guilt, shame, pride, regrets etc. before the therapy actually starts. People report great relief after such forced writing.

It is strongly recommended to write down, at least once a week, all things that we can be grateful for. People have reportedly kept such journals for years, many of them listing more than twenty thousand blessings. This enhances awareness of and appreciation for things we routinely ignore. A shift in consciousness happens which brings a sense of abundance in place of lacking. Feelings like envy and jealousy, which people so commonly harbor, begins to dissolve; you cannot be grateful and resentful at the same time.

There is an interesting pattern seen in many people who maintain a gratitude journal. After initial few days, journaling fatigue sets in. Regular writings starts looking difficult. This is the moment when they need a nudge to continue the exercise. Gradually, it becomes a self-fulfilling process which helps in resolving conflicts making life more peaceful. Journaling must be done with a sense of deep involvement. It cannot be treated like an item on your "to do list".

Following points are important in journaling:

i. Be specific. Don't just write platitudes like I am grateful to my mother. Recall how many times she hugged you, the countless times she fed you and dropped you to school. In Indian society, it is estimated, that a child is fed 20,000 times by her mother. Try and identify other things you received as gift e.g. the clothes, the medicines, the books or the love she gave while nurturing you. These are all gifts which will enhance the beauty of journaling.

ii. Surprise element (whether pleasant or otherwise) amplifies the emotional impact. All factors being equal, unexpected events produce stronger emotional reaction than those anticipated. Accordingly, they bring greater joy or sorrow as the case may be. On the contrary when something expected happens, people do not feel as grateful even though they had strongly desired it. Factor in this fact while deciding items for writing.

iii. The way we think is more important than what we think - and our ways are indeed strange. For example, we remain oblivious to the possibility of losing everything without being warned in advance. It is not recognized that the most beautiful moments can turn ugly in the blink of an eye. A perfect vacation can be ruined by illness, an accident or air tickets booked on a wrong flight. But are we ever grateful when nothing untoward happens during the holiday? Perhaps never. That is because we routinely take things as given. We want more of good things to come our way in the present moment and pay no attention to the fact that many bad things, which could have happened, did not happen. Writing these in the diary will certainly help. Appreciating 'what is' becomes easy if we learn to keep stock of what could have gone wrong.

**2. Negative visualizations**

It is useful to remember that every good thing in your life will come to an end. Everything that appears shall disappear too. Since we have an innate tendency to bury unpleasant thoughts in deeper recesses of our mind, negative visualization has to be forced. Imagine you are going to die in the next 48 hours. Feel it as intensely as possible. Now, make a list of the persons who have helped you in life. Would you like to acknowledge their contributions by thanking them before you die? This thought experiment enables us to internalize mortality making it possible for us to capitalize on what remains. Gratitude frequency increases if we start appreciating our possessions before they are actually lost to the vagaries of time.

It is common to find people who lament at not having lived fully with a person who was close to them but is now dead. This regret will accentuate the gnawing vacuum arising out of death. For them, it is too late now. To experience it, imagine someone you love has died. Think it as vividly as you can. Feel the loss and imagine the sorrow it will bring. Identify things, actions and words that should not have been postponed. Because after the person is no more, the regret of not having done these things will bring suffering. This practice may sound depressing but is necessary to experience reality of life. The importance of people, things and situations will increase manifold when we realize that their existence is for a limited time. It brings a new beauty to our relationship.

Remember there is always a last time when you do a particular thing. For example, remember the time you last met your late father or went to school for the parent-teacher meet? When you do anything like say, boarding a train or driving your car or eating in a restaurant, tell yourself that this is the last time you are doing it. As this recognition sinks in, the perspective will shift making what was hitherto trivial and routine suddenly become significant. You will notice a new beauty and fragrance embrace the heart warmly. It will become easier to recognize and name this feeling 'gratitude' as it grows.

### 3. Expressing in person

Select a person who has made a positive difference in your life but you have never thanked him for it. Write a one-page note about his contribution, while expressing your gratitude. Do not hurry. Savor every word you write and take as long as you want – few hours or even days. Then visit him and request it to be read in your presence. Research shows that such a visit bring lasting happiness compared to many other interventions. We must also learn to appreciate service providers – the sweeper, driver, teacher, vegetable vendor etc. Everyone loves to hear words of genuine thanks. Recognize as many individuals as you can, who have benefited you in any way – material, emotional, social or spiritual. Be thankful to them.

### 4. Spiritual practices

The dictionary meaning of the word spiritual is 'relating to or affecting the human spirit as opposed to material or physical things. This spirit is the energy we have referred to repeatedly in this book. We have learnt about the blockages and the need to dissolve them in order to maximize the flow of energy. A spiritual practice in this context refers to a set of exercises that help dissolve obstructing fragments and thus open up the heart. As a consequence, the emotional system gets purged of feelings like hatred, jealousy, envy, resentment, guilt and shame. Such a clean heart slows down the mind and punctuates the otherwise incessant chattering. This is essentially a meditative state.

Spiritual practices have been a source of much debate and confusion. Different people pursue them with different goals in mind. Some want to connect with the spirit world (presuming it exists), others aim at experiencing visions of future and many aspire to attain 'Samadhi' or liberation. The claims of mystical experiences through spiritual exercises can be contested and may fail to meet stringent standards of scientific inquiry. However if explored deeply enough, it is easy to recognize that many spiritual Sadhnas (act of training oneself in a particular discipline) in almost all major traditions create a deep sense of gratitude. Let's study some of them.

### a) Fasting

The significance of things which are routinely available is never understood till they are denied to us. This was realized by millions during the country wide lockdown in March 2020 following the spread of Covid-19 pandemic. Everything we take for granted like travel, medical treatment, working in the office, eating in restaurants etc. was suddenly taken away. The significance of all these things became loud and clear (sadly most of us have already forgotten it).

Almost all religions recommend fasting – a voluntary decision not to eat (or even drink) for a particular period of time. Ten days after new year in Judaism, the holy month of Ramadan in Islam, the Navratras (nine nights) in Hinduism are all devoted to fasting. People fast for all reasons – spiritual, psychological and physical. The importance of food and water is magnified by this temporary deprivation. It sharpens the smell, sight and flavor of food – something which does not happen in routine life. It makes you mindful of every morsel you eat. You savour it like never before. The gnawing hunger enables us to see food as a blessing – an invaluable gift.

Fasting teaches us not to take food for granted. It shows that eating is not just a routine, but an occasion to be grateful for.

**b) Silence**

Ordinarily, to observe silence means to stop speaking voluntarily for a specific period of time. By itself it is a powerful exercise. But it is only first step in the process of mastering the art of becoming truly silent. In the second step communication in any form – whether with words, through writing or gestures including eye-contact is given up. The use of TV, books or listening to or conversing with other people is also prohibited. Communication (interaction) with other people keeps us so distracted that we miss the rhythm of life. Silence makes you mindful and things hitherto ignored start appearing in our consciousness. It revives energy levels and enhances awareness. The ability to see the bounties around improves. The practices to cultivate gratitude produce better results if they are done in silence.

It may be noted that the silence described above is physical in nature and it does not stop the chattering of the partner. Thoughts continue to appear either as images or through verbalization and we continue to oscillate between the past and the future relentlessly.

### c) Meditation

The physical silence mentioned above is easy to observe but there is a deeper silence within. It is there by itself and not by virtue of any practice. It cannot be disturbed because there is no 'you' there. It simply is and therefore can only be recognized but cannot be practiced. It is the core of our being – a space where personality, idea of being a doer does not exist. It is the seat of pure awareness – aware of all that arises in it. The access to this supremely silent space becomes possible only when the clouds of thoughts disperse. Anyone entering this realm is essentially in a meditative state.

Very often the word 'meditation' is used loosely and inaccurately. Ordinarily, it is understood as a set of techniques deployed for resting the mind and experiencing a state of higher consciousness. Meditation is not an act of doing something. It is a state of being in which thoughts including the thought of thoughtlessness peter out. Thus meditation begins where the mind ends. It reveals our true nature and is experienced as deep sense of peace, prayerfulness and gratitude.

Meditation and silence are two sides of the same coin. When gratitude fills up the heart, it makes one silent, meditative and prayerful. Each day we must find time and make effort to recall something good that happened. Do not look for materially significant achievements but simple things like someone having smiled at you or that the day passed without anything untoward incident. This can fill-up the heart with love. Keep looking for people, situations, experiences for which you can be thankful. Don't look for only the good. The bad also has a lesson to offer provided you are open to receiving it. The moment we feel gratitude the situation begins to lighten up. It helps in overcoming fear, inoculating us against worry, diluting resentment and dissolving anguish. Gratitude energizes, heals and rejuvenates us. Life begins to draw people and circumstances for whom you would be grateful.

Gratitude cuts through all life-situations, socio-cultural conditionings and religious beliefs to expose the beauty of human core. Anyone who has learnt the art of living in gratitude will never experience dearth of good in life. His list of plenty shall indeed be endless.

## Gratitude and the blockages

We learnt in Chapter 2-The Space Within (Part One) how the energy of stimulus which does not pass through seeks release through an emotional upsurge. If this rising is unpleasant, we instinctively avoid it; if it is pleasant, we instinctively hold it. By shoving it aside or clinging to this upsurge, the energy of disturbance gets trapped within the system. This stuck energy, which is like a small cloud of smoke that is unable to find a passage for escape, is called an 'impression'. It carries all details of thoughts, feelings and images related to an event and stays as such for decades. For example an 'impression' formed by a childhood abuse can, many years later, bring to surface the associated fear and insecurity. The euphoria of winning a keenly contested competition or making a discovery can also be relived any time in life. This happens because there is a corresponding 'impression' which can be stimulated. We add to the existing stock of impressions, simply by averting or adhering to an experience, on a daily basis without realizing the ramifications. Nature builds a protective shield around the 'impression' so that their contents do not pop up in awareness. Imagine countless impressions releasing details of experience stored in them at random. It will drive anyone insane. The shielded impressions, called 'fragments', continue to grow in numbers. They work as blockages obstructing the flow of energy through the heart thereby making us feel low. They are the seeds of suffering we sow every day.

Let us examine how a man who lives in gratitude responds to a situation. Energy of an unpleasant event kick starts a disturbance within. It can gather force and grow in intensity if awareness is sucked in. In the case of a man who lives in gratitude, the awareness remains sharply focused on the existing good and the plenty around. It is strongly tethered to abundance and will not be easily available for getting drawn into the disturbance. As a consequence, the energy of the stimulus does not face any resistance or clinging and will, therefore, pass through without creating an impression. The result is very profound – the world around loses the power to clog the heart.

Gratitude thus creates a condition in which the heart does not close. It helps the energy within to flow freely essentially making life joyful. Thus as a navigator, gratitude will always make you turn in the right direction.

## IN GRATITUDE

*In gratitude, in gratitude*
*In gratitude I live.*
*For all the blessings*
*that you did give.*

*Countless gifts you bestowed*
*and took away all my loads.*
*Gave me roof and bread to eat*
*gave me kin whom I can greet.*

*A pillow to sleep*
*and friends to keep.*
*Gave me a mind that can think*
*and the hands that can link.*

*I thank you for the Stars*
*Moon and the Sun.*
*I thank you for all*
*the laurels I have won.*

*Thank you for the valleys and hills*
*for the beautiful wasp on my Sill.*
*I thank you for the foggy Shrouds*
*of fluffy, Soft, milky Clouds.*

*I thank you for the birds that*
*Sing and for little kids on the Swings.*
*My gratitude for Oceans and the Streams*
*and for the vision and my dreams.*

*In gratitude for your love and care*
*for accomplishments that I could dare.*
*I thank you for lifting the veils*
*where awakening, realization reigns.*

*Thank you for my smiles and tears*
*for the reassuring words that I hear.*
*I thank the wind as it sweeps*
*thank you for my peaceful sleep.*

*Thank you for the hope you gave*
*to see yet another morning's ray.*
*In gratitude as you guide and save*
*for all the riches that you gave.*

(From collection of poems **"Till I become you"** by Harkirat)

# R FOR RESPONSIBILITY

## Chapter 6

# R For Responsibility

The dictionary meaning of the word 'Responsibility' is:

*"A duty to deal with or take care of somebody/ something so that you may be blamed if something goes wrong."*

We carry different sets of responsibilities on our shoulders depending on the role being played. For example, as parents, friends, citizens and business entities we are responsible for bringing up children, offering them support in need, observing the law of the land and dealing honestly with the customers respectively. Sometimes we willingly own responsibilities; but there are moments when we feel they have been forced upon us. There are some duties that we discharge satisfactorily; whilst there are many, which for various reasons, are not performed. Generally speaking a responsible behavior is socially appreciated and rewarded.

Our intentions and actions are influenced by people, situations and motivations. The architects of modern civilization clearly understood that if humans are given total freedom they would follow their animal instincts. It was therefore necessary to establish formal ways of ensuring responsible behavior – one that meets social approbation. So a set of rules governing social conduct came into existence making it possible to keep order in society. Their compliance was achieved through a system of rewards and penalties. Broadly speaking, there were two types of rules.

i. Those governed directly by law enforcing agencies

ii. Those governed by existing socio-religious order.

The formal legal system administered rules of the first kind while divine retribution and social reprimand was used to enforce the rules of the second kind. In theocratic regimes, it was not easy to keep the two set of rules apart. Irrespective of the nature of the regulatory regime, societies have rewarded those abiding by these laws and held them in esteem. We easily understand the concept of responsibility in the context of the outer world. It is clearly related with the familial, societal, national or global duties mentioned above.

However, the idea of responsibility, that we intend to study in this chapter, has no relationship with the worldly duties we perform each day. It is about the extent to which we are responsible for what happens in the space-within or the so called 'inner world'.

## What does responsibility mean in the context of the 'inner world'?

In the context of the inner world, to be responsible means that the way we feel at any given moment depends entirely on us and nobody else. This is a very simple yet powerful fact. Somehow, our up-bringing, educational system and cultural foundation does not pay any attention to it. That is why most of us believe that the world, i.e. people, situations and events, are the root cause of the way we feel at a given point in time. We spend lot of time and energy in setting them right in order to feel better. This is trying to find solution outside for a problem which is actually inside. The tragedy is that we do not recognize how adversely this approach affects the quality of our life.

Whether we like it or not, the fact is that, in general, the world around is not interested in our wants. It works according to its own laws and priorities without regard to anybody's preferences. A dog might bark when you are asleep peacefully, a flash flood can sweep away all that you saved for old age and a friend may refuse to help when you needed it the most. Most of us do not really realize how uncertain life can be until something untoward – illness, accident, failure or calamity – happens. We continue to make complex arrangements for physical, financial, professional and social security. There is a constant struggle to find some permanent foothold in a world that is fundamentally impermanent.

*The suffering does not arise because things outside are not in our control, but actually stems from the fact that what happens within us is not in our control.*

Let us check some facts. Our sensory system receives stimulus enabling us to see, hear, smell, touch and taste. If all these inputs are perceived just the way they are, life would be free from inner disturbances. But that does not happen. There are other things that happen simultaneously. For example, take the case of Raveena, a young divorcee, whose ex-husband was very passionate about the red SUV he owned. One day an identical car happened to pass by. It was like any other red car on the road which did not deserve any special notice. The visual energy of the car should have passed through like all other sights on the road. But that did not happen. The car brought back memories of courtship and subsequent marriage to her ex-husband bringing tears to her eyes. On some other day, the sight of the same red car might rekindle memories of marital violence and the pain of going through the divorce proceedings. This time Raveena may be filled with rage instead of tears. The same sensory input (sight of a red car) is processed in totally different ways on two different occasions. Obviously, she was looking through the glasses of memory – it was not purely a physical act of seeing. The way a stimulus is processed and perceived is a very complex. So 'what is' can be completely different from what appears on the mind-screen. Thus the drama enacted on your internal private stage bears no relation to what happened outside. The world is perceived the way it is being projected within. This means that an event is not seen and felt identically by two different persons because they process it differently. So, a single reality is converted into as many realities as the number of people looking at it.

As stated above, an event outside can be projected inside the same person in totally different ways on different occasions. Similarly a particular event will affect different people in totally different ways. This is 'Maya' that people very often speak about in India. It alludes to an illusion; one which does not let you see the reality as 'it is'. Maya is an outcome of the pull exercised on awareness by the ripples created by a stimulus. It makes us blind to the truth. After all, it was only a red car outside; but it refused to be seen purely as a red car inside. The outcome was tears on one occasion and rage the other time. Unfortunately, this is considered absolutely normal. Ask anyone why Raveena was pained to see a red car. The reply will invariably be:

"She must have suffered a lot at the hands of her husband. Such personal experiences leave permanent scars. It is not possible to forget such trauma." These explanations look innocuous, convincing and makes a sympathetic conversation. The entire idea of blaming others for our pain is convenient and obvious. This is why the drama that happened inside is narrated by Raveena in the language of blame – she acts like a victim of the conditions created by the marriage. In such situation it is common to hear remarks like "He was an insensitive man who couldn't care less for me. He wrecked my life". Clearly the emotional strife was controlling her life.

It is common to hear people say:

"My neighbor provoked me."

"I resent the way my husband treats me."

"I got angry with my manager."

Whom are we holding responsible for the provocation, resentment and anger in the above statements? Obviously the neighbor, husband and the manager. That things happening outside are not under our control is easy to understand. But is it not strange that what happens inside also not under our control? If that is not the case, why would the person making the above statements be agonized? But is it right to blame others and hold them responsible for how we feel in a given moment? To find an answer let us imagine someone standing in front of you inquires

"Who is in there?"

You will say "It is me."

"Who else is there with you?" he says again.

"No one" you reply.

This "me" receives the stimulus through sense organs, recalls stored memories, passes judgments, creates grudges and feels happy on achieving a goal. Since by your own admission there is nobody else in there everything that is created, recreated or modified is actually being done by you. After all, if a person is the only one living in a house, wouldn't he be responsible for keeping it the way it is? He cannot blame the neighbor if the house is in shambles. This choice to keep our house 'within' in a particular state is the greatest freedom we have. Unfortunately we do not recognize this and think that the world is answerable for the condition it is in. So we blame people for our psychological mess. This is a tragic situation.

*Jhumroo opened his lunch box in the office and found a loaf of bread inside. He shared it with his friend who had brought delicious food. Next day he found bread again in the tiffin. He got wild on the third day when he again discovered bread in the box. He called names and threatened to divorce his wife the same evening.*

*"Why are you so upset" said the wise friend who shared lunch each afternoon in the office "just tell whosoever prepares your lunchbox to cook something different each day. By the way who packs your lunchbox?"*

*"Well... actually... you know... I do it myself" said Jhumroo sheepishly.*

Look what Jhumroo is doing. He packed his lunch himself every day but blames his wife for the bad menu. It is easy to laugh at his foolishness but difficult to admit that in real life all of us do the same each day. We pack anger, hatred, envy, fear and guilt within but very conveniently hold others responsible for it. Somehow we genuinely believe that somebody else is packing our lunchbox whereas actually we do it ourselves. Jhumroo is wise; at least he knew who was packing his lunchbox every day.

We are pleased when people do certain things; and get upset when they do certain other things. This happens because we expect them to do things according to our likes and dislikes. When that does not happen, and which is very often the case, we get disappointed. This is considered normal and natural. The fact is otherwise. Although there is nothing wrong in keeping expectations, but it is certainly wrong to think that unpleasantness is inevitable when they are not met. A person, thing or situation cannot force you to feel a particular way unless you allow it. You have the freedom to choose the response – much like the fact that you are free to pack the lunch of your choice unless somebody else is allowed to decide the menu and pack it. Unfortunately, we are not trained to exercise this choice and much of our suffering is rooted in this incompetence. When we say that another person has made me feel in a particular way (pleasant or unpleasant), we are surrendering the freedom to choose our feelings to such 'other'. Sadly most of us do not even know that such freedom exists and that we have surrendered it.

*One day Jhumroo was driving. The traffic police stopped him and issued a ticket of Rs 500 for over speeding. "Actually I got late trying to get the headlights repaired. The mechanic couldn't make them functional." He explained the reason of hurrying. "Oh! you are travelling without headlights." and the officer issued another ticket for Rs 500. "Haven't I told you to keep shut when you are drunk" said Jhumroo's wife frustrated with the delay. The officer pulled him out of the car "I can't let you drive while you are drunk" and slapped another fine. "Hey! Officer' cried Jhumroo "She sits next to me and keeps telling when to speed, turn or stop. I only hold the steering: she is the one actually driving. Please ask her to pay up."*

In one sense we are all Jhumroos. We claim to live freely, but actually allow others to steer us. That is why these 'others' make us angry, miserable or happy and we helplessly fall victim to their machinations. The consequences can be disastrous. Why does road rage occur when an unknown person overtakes a car from the wrong side? Why does your temper begins to rise when a loud music is played in the neighborhood? The reason is simple – instead of maneuvering the car, you are only sitting behind the driving wheel. You have preferred to be a victim of a situation and are not willing to be its master. Being responsible means to be in control. It is all about you; others have no role to play in it.

## Pen picture of responsible living

The following story depicts how people respond when they learn to be responsible.

*One day I took a taxi from the airport. After a short while, a car suddenly jumped out of a side lane. My driver slammed on brakes just in time to avert a disaster. The man in the other car not realizing what he had done, rolled down the window and howled at us. My cab driver smiled back and waved. I asked him* "The fellow almost sent us to the hospital and you smiled back."

*"Some people are like a garbage truck." he explained, "They run around full of rubbish (resentment, jealousy, hatred, anger). As these pile up, they need a place to dump it. And sometimes they may dump it on you. By smiling at him, I refused to take it."*

By not choosing to be responsible, you become a dumping ground. All our resentment, annoyance, envy etc. is the stench of this garbage which others keep pouring on us.

Since every mind is conditioned in a unique way, therefore its response to a given stimulus is also unique. It needs courage, self-discipline and commitment to erase old grooves and create new patterns in their place. Learning new things by unlearning the old ones is indeed difficult. It is much easier to wear a garb instead of effecting an authentic change. When responsible men stop blaming others, it is not a put on. They effectively modify the default settings of their neural network. The way they think and respond is transformed.

We are repeatedly taught values like obedience to parents, honesty in profession, kindness to others, and respecting the elders. These are basically expectations and anyone who fails to meet them is put to shame. The idea is to develop a sense of guilt in someone who defies these values which works as a deterrent against repetition of the slip-up. In place of authentic moral living such strategy spawns hypocrisy. The good behavior is reduced to only a garb that projects an amiable appearance. It is not natural and instinctive. In trying circumstances this mask of goodness falls apart exposing the true ugliness underneath. This sad state of affairs has come about because societies did not understand the power of responsibility to transform human life. A responsible man regains the authority to govern his inner world. Whatever be the life situation, he gets affected only to the extent he decides. This is freedom – to be able to stay unmoved in both good and bad times. His happiness ceases to be at the mercy of what others do. This servility ends because he does not see others as the cause of his emotional state. In one sense, he has learnt to treat himself sensitively and lovingly. So, to say "I am responsible" means "I love myself." It is like mothering oneself. Eventually, you become your own best friend.

For any society maintaining order is of paramount importance. Imposing a code of conduct based on certain set of values is one way of achieving this. Forcing people to learn ethics and behave accordingly is much easier than teaching them to be responsible. We do not make institutional efforts to transform people by changing their mental patterns. The perseverance and understanding necessary to obtain is not an easy investment. That is why something as valuable as 'living responsibly' did not find any place amongst the values that are cherished in different parts of the world. It is not surprising that it is neither a part of our educational curriculum nor the cultural ethos.

## Biological impact of not living responsibly

The "fight, flight or freeze" (3F) response is a gift of

evolutionary forces. It helps us to face life threatening situations by releasing stress hormones like adrenaline and cortisol to prepare the body for fighting back. The brain shunts blood away from the gut and moves it towards the muscles in preparation for the physical exertion. The heart rate, blood pressure, glucose levels and respiratory rate increases. The alertness of the mind is heightened and focus sharpens. This instinct is essential for the survival of the Homo sapiens race.

Over time the issue of physical survival lost primacy because technology provided a reasonably safe and secure life. But increasing complexities of structured societies, cultural expectations and multiple activities began to pose psychological threats. The yelling of the boss, treachery of a friend, peer disapproval and public defamation began to create intimidating situations. The body knows only one way to escape from threats, whether physical or psychological, and that is by triggering the 3F response. Every emotional threat induces this response and the consequent metabolic changes, as mentioned above, happen as many times. It works like a 'slow poison' and eventually immense harm is caused to the human body.

Take the case of anger. Research shows that it can cause the following problems:

i. Anxiety

ii. Insomnia

iii. Depression

iv. High blood-pressure

v. Heart attack

vi. Headache

vii. Stroke

viii. Gastro-intestinal problems

ix. Skin problems, such as eczema

Those who choose anger as their response to life situations are in fact inviting these diseases. Anger may scare others to become more compliant and improve their performance. One cannot be sure if that happens every time we blow our top. But it is certain that anger increases the level of toxins in the biological system. Is it not consuming slow poison?

All other emotions like guilt, shame, fear, grief and despair that bring some kind of psychological threat will affect the biology in the same way as anger does.

## Why do people think 'living responsibly' is a bad idea?

It is counterintuitive to say that other people cannot be blamed for hurting us. Our conventional thinking suggests that this can happen only when we become stone-like to remain unaffected by what others do to us. After all humans are social beings and they connect through affection and respect. The social order depends on how men conduct their relations with others. That is why it is considered important to treat others sensitively lest they get hurt.

In order to make people accountable for their actions, strategies like "Tit for Tat" and "an eye for an eye" have found wide acceptance. It is strongly argued that not holding people responsible for how they make others feel, is an invitation to endless humiliation and exploitation. It is fraught with serious danger of losing both human dignity and material goods. Derisively, they portray a 'responsible' person as someone who is silently seated in lotus position while the world pours muck on him. The idea of teaching people to be responsible, in this sense, is fraught with risk of creating lawlessness in the society.

It is also argued that responsible people will not be affected by what others do (whether good and bad) therefore, they will not resist misconduct nor appreciate mature behavior. It would be impossible to keep order in a society where people are immune to what is happening around them. Even universally accepted values like kindness and compassion will become irrelevant. This is an unsafe social condition in which enforcement of a code of conduct would be difficult. The possibility of men becoming uncivilized looks real. The social order would be severely stressed, civilization jeopardized and we may go back to the days of jungle laws.

## Is it correct to say that 'living responsibly' is a bad idea?

The arguments against the idea of living responsibly holds a strong appeal especially to those who have not personally experienced it. Ordinarily people cannot envisage the profound quietness of the space in which a responsible man lives. At an intellectual level, and most of us cannot go beyond that, it can easily be presented as 'passive living'. However, at experiential level the fact is absolutely different.

The thoughts and emotions wandering on the streets of your inner world behave in much the same manner as a restive crowd on the road. Imagine a situation where an agitated mob gathers in a marketplace. The police officer on the spot looks the other way, hoping it will not go berserk. His apparent indifference towards the situation can have serious repercussions on the safety and security of citizens. The crowd has no respect for his optimism and therefore it would not be surprising if it goes on a rampage. A responsible police officer on the other hand, will not turn his back on such a grave situation. He feels duty bound to keep the restive crowd under control, whether by persuasion or by force. Then he takes steps necessary to restore order. Most of the times even simple demonstration of the willingness to act is enough for a peaceful dispersal of the crowd.

The horde of thoughts and the emotional havoc they wreak behave in much the same way as the crowd on the street outside does. If we hold ourselves accountable, like an alert police officer, the stage is set for their peaceful dispersal. Our capacity to handle thoughts and emotions increases manifold when we begin to face them with increasing confidence and awareness. With regular practice, it is possible to gain the competence of watching them closely. They can be seen appearing and dispersing as well. In this state of being, thoughts and emotions are rendered incapable of overwhelming. The energy simply passes through. This is the state in which a responsible man lives.

To argue that 'to be responsible' means 'to be passive,' and it would encourage people to act unkindly is absolutely fallacious. By deciding to be responsible for our inner state, we do not lose capacity to chastise wrongdoers. Instead, we begin to deal with all situations from a quiet place. There is no habituated reaction of settling a score or teach somebody a quick lesson. There is no emotional turbulence – like anger, hatred or fear – to cloud our vision. There is no urge to act against a wrong doer out of a burning sense of vengeance. An unprovoked mind can see all dimensions of the issue clearly and is therefore well equipped to take a balanced view. Thus, a responsible man will take action to remedy the situation in a befitting manner. The decision made and action taken against a misdemeanor will befit the circumstances.

By default, a responsible man chooses not to let his awareness get carried away by people, situations and things. He remains centered and therefore unfazed. His psyche does not process inputs in a habituated or mechanical way. Instead, it is like a mirror which keeps reflecting the happenings faithfully. In this condition the psyche does not get hurt, unlike what routinely happens to us. Consequently feelings like jealousy, hatred, anger and guilt do not take roots in him. A responsible man operates from a place of innate human goodness personifying the ultimate in ethical living, even without taking formal lessons in moral education. It fills him up with unconditional love for others. Authentic compassion is born out of this.

All this explaining notwithstanding, most of us may still feel that responsibility is not a workable idea. Some of us may comment "Not everyone can be a Buddha. It is not possible for ordinary mortals to cultivate awareness needed to achieve it". Others may ask, "How can anyone watch every disturbance occurring within without retorting?" These seemingly convincing queries conveniently ignore the power of practice which makes it possible. Remember the first time you sat behind the steering wheel of a car. Initially the coordination necessary for smooth driving looks difficult. With sufficient practice, we start driving with ease even in busy traffic while listening to the music or discussing plans with others. Likewise, a child repeatedly falls when he begins to take the first baby steps. But that does not stop him from trying. If the child gives up or the mother discourages him from trying to walk, he would become severely disabled for the rest of the life. It is only because everyone continues to help him learn how to walk that, one day, he might run in the Olympics. In much the same way, with consistent efforts we can raise awareness to levels necessary for cultivating responsibility. It may be difficult, but not impossible.

## What needs to be done to become responsible?

The answer is simple – first be sensitive to every shift in the energy that takes place within you. This basically means to develop the ability to identify the moment when a change in the way one is feeling happens. Second, move the attention immediately from the object (which caused the shift) to the subject (i.e. you). Say, you are having coffee with your fiancée when a friend calls up to inform that your father has met with an accident. The way you feel will suddenly change. This is what is called the shift in energy. Pause and watch what is happening in your heart. You will notice the rise of worry and fear. If you do not wish to be carried away by the news and its suddenness, keep your attention focused on yourself i.e. the sensations and feelings arising in your body. The degree of resolve and awareness required to be able to do this is not easy to acquire. Initially, everyone falters – very much like the child who keeps falling in his initial attempts to walk, but with practice it learns. The key is not to stop doing it, come what may. It will be difficult in times of extreme emotional state (like deep grief and also exuberance) but most other situations are quite ordinary. By shifting attention, you are announcing "I am responsible for this emotional disturbance." Actually it is less of saying and more of feeling deeply. With enough practice as you gain the necessary skill, the whole exercise becomes effortless. It lays a strong foundation of equanimity which improves quality of life enormously. But remember, it will not happen by reading this book or listening to an erudite speaker. It requires a different kind of training, one that is never imparted – training to use awareness to keep the heart open.

Remember how a child is taught to safely cross the road? You tell him to Stop-look-go. This principle also applies to any training aimed at making you responsible. You first learn to pause. Bring all activities – like dining, listening to music, walking – to a halt for a short time. This is 'stop'. Withdraw all your attention from them and bring it on the sensations in the body. This is to 'look' – essentially trying to examine the rising feelings. After a minute or two resume the activity you were performing-this is 'go'. Deepen this practice to develop the skill necessary to shift awareness from object to subject (yourself) in real life situations. It becomes possible to stop-look-go whenever something unpleasant happens.

People do all kinds of things to be at peace like going to temples, praying, reading scriptures, memorizing verses, listening to sermons and attending meditation classes. All these activities may help (much like avoidance) but they do not offer any permanent solution. Unless efforts to become responsible are made in true earnest, the results will never be satisfactory. Our daily life is the best laboratory where all kinds of experiments can be done. It offers innumerable opportunities of skilling ourselves in becoming responsible.

It is interesting to observe that negative emotions dissipate when attention shifts from object to subject. But love and joy becomes more intense. Instead of melting away, they amplify and take deeper roots. This is a matter of experience. Sharp observation is needed to test the truth of this assertion.

All cigarette packs carry the statutory warning "Smoking is injurious to health". People read the warning and claim to understand what it means and still pull out a cigarette and light it up. All the understanding does not stop us from smoking. Why?

Because your reading and comprehension is limited to just words. The fatal injury that smoking can inflict is not immediate and therefore the warning is perceived by us more as a potential threat than a real one. If you had really understood the harm it might eventually bring, even if in remote future, smoking would become impossible. So simply reading the warning "smoking is injurious" is different from knowing the same. Why do you choose a glass of wine over a glass of poison if both are offered to you? Because you clearly "know" which one would definitely kill you. This is real knowing and not an understanding of any intellectual concept. Similarly, no one becomes responsible by reading the statement like: "Watch closely how thoughts and emotions move in the space within". To be able to 'watch', we need to seriously practice appropriate techniques. As the experience deepens your response to the events of daily life changes. You begin to take the right actions effortlessly. It becomes as simple as choosing wine over poison.

## Responsibility and Blockages

We learnt in Chapter 2-The Space Within (Part One) how the energy of stimulus which does not pass through seeks release through an emotional upsurge. If this rising is unpleasant, we instinctively avoid it; if it is pleasant, we instinctively hold it. By shoving it aside or clinging to this upsurge, the energy of disturbance gets trapped within the system. This stuck energy, which is like a small cloud of smoke that is unable to find a passage for escape, is called an 'impression'. It carries all details of thoughts, feelings and images related to an event and stays as such for decades. For example an 'impression' formed by a childhood abuse can, many years later, bring to surface the associated fear and insecurity. The euphoria of winning a keenly contested competition or making a discovery can also be relived any time in life. This happens because there is a corresponding 'impression' which can be stimulated. We add to the existing stock of impressions, simply by averting or adhering to an experience, on a daily basis without realizing the ramifications. Nature builds a protective shield around the 'impression' so that their contents do not pop up in awareness. Imagine countless impressions releasing details of experience stored in them at random. It will drive anyone insane. The shielded impressions, called 'fragments', continue to grow in numbers. They work as blockages obstructing the flow of energy through the heart thereby making us feel low. They are the seeds of suffering we sow every day.

Let us now understand how responsible living affects the formation of these blockages. A responsible person is the master of his inner world. He responds to the outside world in accordance with his express wish. This is made possible by the elevated level of awareness he possess which helps him to identify the shift in energy the moment it happens. This is the moment in which a stimulus has just begun to cause disturbance. He is quick to move his focus from the object (cause of pain) to his own space within (subject) so that the disturbance can be closely observed. He is sharp at noticing sensations and feelings in the body-mind complex. This simple watching disengages awareness from the powerful pull of disturbance, allowing the energy of the event to pass through. There is no resistance or clinging, and therefore impressions are not created.

Responsible men do not fall victim to the trappings of habituated responses of the deep mental patterns. So, events that could have otherwise created blockages, leave no residual impression in responsible men. Their heart does not get clogged.

Responsibility is therefore a powerful tool for keeping the heart open. It helps the energy to flow freely which essentially makes us joyful. Thus as a navigator, it will always make you turn in the right direction.

# A FOR ACCEPTANCE

# Chapter 7

# A For Acceptance

The dictionary meaning of the word "Acceptance" is:

*"A general agreement that something is satisfactory or right/the act of agreeing to an offer, plan or invitation."*

The common understanding is that there is an element of satisfaction about the object of acceptance and agreeing to it as well. Actually that is not so. In fact it is a powerful tool that brings psychological conflicts to an end. Therefore, the scope, meaning and interpretation of the word acceptance is much wider than is normally construed. This chapter is an attempt to understand what acceptance is from the point of view of joyful living.

## What does acceptance mean

Take a simple situation. You are driving to a friend's

house to attend a dinner party. It is raining heavily. Suddenly the car skids off the road and into the muddy sidewalk. All your driving skills to extricate the stuck car fail. As you sit helplessly, anger may start rising drawing more of your awareness. You start blaming the rain, the car and may be even your wife who pushed you to attend the party. This will neither improve nor worsen the situation but will certainly make planning retrieval of the car difficult. An agitated mind is always busy regretting, fretting and fuming. But as you let go, cribbing or complaining will peter out. Now the same mind becomes quiet. It can now conceive a quicker and workable solution.

Acceptance means not to rave and rant when the allegorical car gets stuck in the mud. The thoughts and emotions (blaming and bickering) cloud the capacity to plan an effective rescue strategy. A mind working from the place of such chaos can never be at its efficient best. Acceptance is quiet acknowledgment of the fact that a particular situation has arisen. It allows us to open up to reality without getting lost in the storm of emotions otherwise produced. We see it the way it is; nothing more and nothing less. There is no clatter of likes and dislikes or agreements and disagreements. In terms of the flow of energy, it creates the condition in which energy of a stimulus can pass through without creating any disturbance within.

People murmur,

"I can't believe this is happening to me."

"I can't understand why it's like this."

"This can't be true."

These are expressions of non-acceptance i.e. a refusal to acknowledge what is happening. The muddy road is a temporary situation and life will return to the old normal in few hours time, irrespective of how badly you handled it. But there can be irreversible conditions which people find difficult to come to terms with. Death is one such example where people start blaming God or the treating doctors. They mentally rewrite the script of the devastating moments in which their dear one had lost life. Many adopt denial as an approach to alleviate pain. This is actually an attempt to lose touch with reality. The resulting gains, if any, are always short-lived.

Such repudiations do not change the ground reality. Acceptance, on the other hand, means acknowledging the fact as it is. All bubbles of imagination, idealizing, expectation and self-delusion will burst. The clarity arising out of this would help in mitigating the condition in the best possible way. So, the first step is to accept a situation before any remedial action is taken.

Today, an average person enjoys far more comforts than the kings of bygone eras. But we do not appreciate this bounty nor do we acknowledge the free gifts of nature like the sun, rain, trees, flowers and air. Non-acceptance has filled up our minds with the noise of comparison, complains and blames. It is precisely this noise which does not allow us to see the abundance we are gifted with and be grateful for it.

Acceptance of anything, whether a person, situation or an event, means:

- To let go of the tendency of reacting to it
- Not to get obsessed with how good or bad it is
- Not to agree or disagree with it
- Not to blame others for it
- Allowing it to be the way it already is

True acceptance has two parts

i. Seeing clearly, and
ii. Holding the experience as it is with compassion.

The first part implies mindfulness – to be aware of what is happening without manipulating the experience in any way. For example, in fear, we feel tightening in the body and an urge to flee. To be mindful means to stay put whatever is arising. This is not easy because there is an inherent tendency of pulling away because it reduces the pain. Even this tendency of pulling away has to be accepted. There should be no tampering with the event i.e. no denying or minimizing of what has occurred.

The second part of acceptance is to relate to what is being perceived in a tender and sympathetic way. There can be aversion to feelings that arise. They have to be embraced with the kindness of a mother holding her child. There is no escape from this approach whether it is fear or grief. The experience has to be acknowledged and honored for a wholehearted and complete acceptance.

## Is Acceptance Consolation

It is important to first understand that acceptance is not consolation.

There is a famous childhood story of 'The Fox and the Grapes' in Aesop's fables.

*A hungry fox in search of some food entered a vineyard. His mouth watered to see juicy grapes hanging down from a vine. Despite desperate efforts, they remained well out of reach. He was very upset for having failed to get a single grape. "Oh! These grapes must be sour" he consoled himself "There is no point in wasting time here. It is good that are out of my reach. If I had eaten these grapes, they would have left a bad taste in my mouth." The fox then left the vineyard to look for food elsewhere.*

The story illustrates how the mind typically undermines the worth of things we do not achieve. But what if the story had not ended there? Say, another fox had entered the vineyard and managed to grab a bunch and the grapes turned out to be really sweet. And suppose, later in the day he meets the first fox and tells him that the grapes are delicious. The first fox had consoled himself by calling them sour. The ground on which that consolation stood crumbled as soon as he heard the other fox describe the grapes as sweet. Now he may

- Call the other fox a liar and continue to live in his make believe world
- Become jealous
- Feel unhappy for not being able to reach the grapes

The possibility of these responses arises because of one simple fact – the first fox did not accept that he was incapable of jumping high enough to reach the grapes. Like the fox, we too refuse to accept many things every single day without realizing how it impacts our psyche.

Consolation not only diverts attention but also brings hope in the heart of the sufferer. Hope sustains but is a poor substitute of the bold acceptance of the situation. That someone has died or lost a limb or has been born with incurable congenital deformity, are situations which can make people inconsolable. There is no hope, no lesson to be learnt and no amount of waiting would improve the condition. In these situations, they draw consolation by attributing tragic events to the play of cosmic forces. Assigning supernatural reasons to irreversible losses is a practical way of handling emotional upheaval. Spiritual concepts like karma, destiny and grace may also come to the rescue of believers. Is this consolation or acceptance? Since these concepts are based on beliefs and not any direct knowing, they are open to doubt. As long as the underlying belief sustains, it works like acceptance. But when a doubt hits, the balance is lost and the person returns to a state of inner turmoil. The answer, therefore, is simple – consolation works like acceptance till such time as the underlying belief prevails.

In certain cases consolation is a good place to begin, but it must end at acceptance. It is true that many a times we cannot do anything about a given condition. However it does not mean that there is no other option. One option that is always available is:

Would you allow the condition to control your life? Or

Would you control your life?

## Myths about Acceptance

Acceptance is a widely misunderstood term. It would be useful to mention few prevailing myths and ascertain facts in this regard.

**Myth #1:** Acceptance means agreeing with what is happening. You somehow make a situation look right and adjust to it.

**Fact:** There are people, things and situations we don't like. For example, when somebody misbehaves, we do not feel good about it.Acceptance does not mean that we should somehow justify the misdemeanor to dilute the intensity, or should not strongly resist it. Acceptance only means to acknowledge that misconduct has happened. The incident should neither be denied nor over emphasized. There is absolutely no cause for coming to terms with it. You only agree to see it exactly the way it happened and experience the feelings it gave rise to. That being so, the question of making it somehow look right does not arise at all.

**Myth #2:** If a situation is accepted, the motivation to change and control it will be lost.

**Fact:** This myth is propagated by those who believe that acceptance of misbehavior means that it has to be tolerated or forgotten about. That is not true as already stated in myth#1. You are free to respond in any manner. Acceptance does not stop you from settling your scores. You can reprimand or penalize the wrong doer in a befitting manner.

When somebody simply states "I am a smoker" while lighting a cigarette, it is plain acceptance. The option of giving up smoking is available. But if he adds "This is the way I am. Take it or leave it" then it becomes an expression of self indulgence. Now the option to quit smoking is not available anymore. So, an act or statement can be considered acceptance only as long as it marks our true location on the map of life. It should leave all options of choosing the direction we wish to move in.

**Myth #3:** Acceptance is the refuge of the weak and a position of failure. It is a place of no choice. It is a disempowering and depressing end to a lost battle.

**Fact:** Acceptance has no relationship with the nature of the incident. It is admitting the truth of what is happening whether it is success or failure, praise or censure. Anyone who is willing to admit "I have lost" is not weak, but wise. It takes courage to accept defeat and stop denying failure. Therefore it cannot be a refuge of the weak. Acceptance is empowering in the sense that it allows you to see every situation clearly. From this vantage point, the next movement can be planned – a new beginning is possible.

## What is it that has to be Accepted

Broadly speaking, we have to accept:

1. People and situations
2. Ourselves

## 1. Accepting People and Situations

### 1.1 Accepting People

Imagine you are watching a movie in a theatre. In a particular scene a gangster abducts a child for ransom. The kid is scared but the rogue continues to torture him. Unable to put up with the growing tension, a man sitting next to you suddenly stands up shouting, "Hey! you can't do that to the child". You would want to pull him down and say, "Sit down and stop shouting. It will not change the scene." So engrossed was this man in the movie that he forgot that his protest would have no bearing on the film unfolding on the screen. It is common to get involved with the movie and identify closely with the characters on the screen. It happens because all our awareness is drawn in by the perfect synchronization of the projected light and voices coming through the sound system. Music further enhances the pull on our attention.

You might call the man, who protested against abduction, insane or just laugh at the way he was carried away. But if you look closely, most of us behave the same way in our daily lives too. For example, when a friend betrays, you are quick to say "I have always been good to him. How could he deceive me?" Is this reaction any different from that of the man in the movie hall? He shouted against the kidnapping without realizing that it would not change anything. Here you are protesting against the betrayal of a friend without understanding that he is free to take his decisions. Wanting the gang not to kidnap and wanting a friend not to deceive are qualitatively the same: fundamentally it amounts to expecting others to behave in a manner that you think is appropriate.

You could have responded differently to the betrayal by saying, "Well that is the way he chose to be. So be it. Let me see what can be done now." There is no blame-slinging. In this approach, you accept the person (your friend) and the betrayal (the situation). This is a position of freedom because you can now choose any role in this fascinating movie called life. You can fight back like a soldier, learn like a student, enjoy like an amused onlooker, win like a hero or suffer like a helpless victim. We are free to act in a befitting manner only when there is no squabbling with the reality of the circumstances.

*There was a monk who used to pose a question to his disciples to meditate on. On request he gave a seeker this question "What do people need?"*

*The seeker was confused on being given this question. He had desired to contemplate on his own spiritual needs and not that of others. After a few hours, he became uncomfortable since the question did not resonate with him. He went back to the monk and pleaded "Please give me a question that is relevant to my spiritual life."*

*"All right, take this one" said the considerate Master. "What do people really need?"*

The seeker was bewildered as this turned out to be worse than before. He thought spiritual journey was a private affair whereas the Master was asking him to find out what others really wanted. Actually by contemplating on this question, the Master expected that the seeker would realize that ultimately every person wants to be joyful. That is the real need and all human actions are inspired by this desire. Have you ever done anything because it is likely to make you miserable? People do not really need wealth, fame, status, power or other accomplishments. They are actually looking for happiness that success in these worldly pursuits appears to provide. Even when people harm others or think ill of them, they are fundamentally looking for a sense of satisfaction and peace that such harm is likely to bring to them. Your friend, who betrayed, was also seeking pleasure by inflicting pain on you.

To see all actions of people in this light makes their authentic acceptance easy.

## 1.2 Accepting Situations

Have you ever thought what made the present moment, as it is right now, possible? Some 13.7 billion years ago big bang, out of which the universe is believed to have emerged, happened. Everything that occurred in all these millennia is collectively responsible for what is appearing in this moment. It is unchangeable and could not have been any different from what it is– whether you like it or not. It is the accumulated result of all actions since the inception of the cosmos. By refusing to accept a situation, we deny the glory and immensity of this fact.

Acceptance stops the exhausting and unproductive war with any situation. To say, "Yes, this is the way it is, whether I want it or not." relaxes something primal in us. By accepting (even if you don't like the thing in question a bit or don't know what to do about it) you arrive at a truthful place. Thereafter, either:

a) The situation begins to change because of some deliberate intervention, or

b) The relationship with the situation begins to change.

Certain situations can be overwhelming. If that is so, acceptance should not be forced. Even otherwise people become scornful if advised to accept something they strongly dislike. "If only you had suffered what I did, you would never ask me to accept such things" they say, making you feel like a villain who has taken sides with their enemy. Therefore, direct statements like "You should accept it" should be avoided. Instead, it is much better to start by saying, "I am sorry. We are with you." and add, "But now, this situation is the way it is." Such statements are suggestive in nature that makes an open discussion possible. They do not convey a feeling that the story has come to an irretrievable end and that no choices are available. After all many a times things going wrong turn out to be a prelude to something exciting and interesting. Nevertheless, it takes a lot of practice to relax around circumstances that we do not like.

## 2. Accepting Ourselves

We are a complex arrangement of body, thoughts and emotions. Therefore accepting ourselves will necessarily mean accepting all these facets of our existence. Let us discuss them in some detail.

### 2.1 Accept your body

We are in the habit of finding faults with our physical appearance. (I am fat/thin/short/dark or have small nose or grey hair etc.) Nobody seems to be satisfied with the way they look. Even those blessed with attractive physical traits are seen trying to improve their looks. The thriving business of cosmetologists is proof enough of this fact.

You are unique and not meant to be like someone else. Therefore, attempts to match any standard of perfect looks, lifestyle, position and status will only bring dissatisfaction. In all these so called self-improvement projects the starting point is the prevailing sense of inadequacy – the feeling of not being good enough. It grows when the tendency to compare with others becomes acute. The perceived flaws in appearance begin to occupy the centre stage of our attention. This can seriously impact relationships, professional performance and social behavior. It manifests in many ways like avoiding intimacy, not taking leadership roles or lacking initiative for fear of rejection. In that sense, it is an invitation to failure, frustration and anxiety.

*One day a king went to the royal garden. He found that the oak tree was unhappy because it wanted to be tall like the pine. The pine tree was drooping sadly because it wanted to bear grapes like the grapevine. He found that the vine was disheartened because it could not blossom like the rose bush. Finally the King saw a rose plant which was fragrant and blooming, "You look so cheerful and joyful" said the King "Tell me what makes you so happy?" The rose replied, "Oh my dear King! I have not achieved anything by myself. I was planted so that roses could bloom. All these years, I tried giving the best roses,*

*I could. Their fragrance kept me joyful."The rose bush did not complain about the thorns it carried nor wanted to be like any other flower in the garden. It only made efforts to be a better rose.*

The lesson is simple yet profound. To be our very best, we must accept our physical appearance unconditionally.

## 2.2 Accept your thoughts

It is said that an average human mind produces 60,000 thoughts on any given day. We are taught to avoid negative thoughts and shun immoral ones. "Think positive" is a good slogan, but a bad advice propagated by those who believe that thoughts can be controlled. If that was possible, we would have filtered all but joyful thoughts. Happiness would not have remained elusive.

Some people believe that if bad thoughts occur, there must be something wrong with them. It is true that all of us have certain natural or learnt inclinations which influence our thinking to varying extents. For example anyone prone to future concerns is likely to have more of worry thoughts. However thoughts do not need prior permission before appearing in our awareness. Take some time to ponder over the following questions:

1. Can you think a thought before it appears?

2. Do you know what would you be thinking two minutes from now?
3. Are you thinking at this moment? If yes, what? Who decided it and when?

How can anything that arrives and leaves on its own define us? There is a common saying that we become what we think. It happens because we identify ourselves completely with our thoughts. Now a thought, which is otherwise powerless, starts driving our life. But if we recognize them as objects distinct from us, like clouds in the sky, they are reduced to simple appearances in awareness.

Acceptance of a thought means to observe it without getting identified with it.

## 2.3 Accept your desires

All mainstream religions Christianity, Buddhism, Hinduism and Islam consider desires to be the cause of human suffering. The fear of desires becoming wild and intense clearly lurks in all religious orders. Many a times it is advised to shun them as if they are evil.This is a serious misunderstanding because cravings, whether worldly or spiritual, cannot be avoided. But people, mislead by socio-cultural preferences, make all kinds of efforts to break the chain of endless wants. When they fail, which is but natural, a deep sense of despair overcomes. It is wrong to call simple pleasures- food, play, entertainment, sexual gratification as urges of a lower order. They are sacred and part of natural instincts. Unfortunately in their attempt to rise to a different plane of consciousness people simply suppress them. By doing so, they get disconnected from the source of life, love and a sense of being alive. After all, desire is a powerful and pervasive drive which impacts the survival of human beings. It makes us eat, work, reproduce and innovate. There is a universal desire for a happy existence. That is why meeting the desires of this mind-body-spirit complex is fulfilling; denying them makes us feel deprived, frustrated and incomplete. By themselves, desires are neither evil nor virtuous. But the trouble starts when they possess the individual and take over his sense of who he is. The question therefore, is not whether you can successfully shun desires or not. It is:

Are you in control of yourself? Or

Are the desires in control of you?

Basic desires are simple and so is the response to them – to drink when thirsty, to eat when hungry and to sleep when tired. But over centuries the human mind evolved in a complex way resulting in emergence of wants of different kinds. For example, most of us want to:

- Feel good at all times whether in job or in relationships
- Be in complete control of our lives
- Control other people

Even though you know pretty well that none of this is possible, you still keep trying. This is because you are not in control, your desires are. You are in control of the desire to eat if it arises when you are hungry. Similarly the want of shelter and clothing is understandable. But if the craving for food is uncontrolled and greed to hoard is compelling, the desires have clearly taken over the control over you. Anyone who has struggled to give up smoking, compulsive overeating or drug addiction knows it very well. In the epic Mahabharta, Duryodhan was blinded by rage when Draupadi described him as 'the blind son of a blind man'. From there on, the desire to avenge humiliation took complete control of him.

Some people suggest that we should limit desires or keep them under control. They advise that we keep restraint by taking as much as we need. It is difficult to define where needs end and greed begins. It is said, "That which can be fulfilled is need, and that which cannot be is greed." But all these notions do not help in clearly stating what should be done, on real time basis, to ensure that we are not controlled by desires.

To ascertain who is in control, we can do the following exercise:

Take a pause. In this pause recognize the presence of a desire and with kindness, allow it to remain just as it is. It is like inviting desire for a cup of tea to spend some time together. Experience the sensations in your body; fully note the emotions and thoughts arising in the presence of this desire. Do not resist it or cling to it. Gradually, the intensity of desire will begin to dissipate.

To illustrate, bring focus of your attention on any compulsive want in a given moment (it could be about food, smoking, alcohol, sex, gossiping, computer gaming etc). Become physically still and pay close attention to what the body feels during this strong wanting. In which part of the body do you experience the sensation of this wanting the most? Observe. It can be felt as butterflies in the stomach, heaviness in the chest, aching in the arms. Check if your mind is chattering or sluggish. Notice if your experience changes during the pause. If after the pause you still feel pushed to fulfill the want, do so slowly and mindfully. Keep noticing the sensation, including the emotion that arises. Do it with clear and compassionate attention. Don't feel low for having pursued the want. At least you have done it with awareness of the underlying urge and the disturbance it was creating. Gradually, this will help you to see the desire up-close and the urge to act on it will begin to wane. A pause is the only way to accept desires and surprisingly it is the key to freedom from desires as well.

Pause should be practiced for at least a week with compulsive behavior like smoking, drinking, abusing and eating junk food or similar undesirable habits.

## 2.4 Accept your fears

Fear plays a very important role in the survival of species. It prepares us to face a threat by tensing the muscles, increasing heart rate and blood pressure, narrowing the vision and increased oxygenation of the brain. In modern-day life, fear can force you to do a variety of things, depending on the underlying need, like staying awake during examinations, making you rush to a cardiologist after a chest pain and making you work overtime to please the boss. It can come in the guise of worry, paranoia, stress, guilt or threat.

Fear has no relation with the present moment because it depends on the way the future is projected. It is the anticipation of pain. The thought of what may go wrong (not what has gone wrong) is the genesis of worry. Since change is inevitable therefore the presence of constant uncertainty can make fear work 24×7. This is a serious condition because even when there is no immediate threat our body will remain tense and mind focused on the possibility of mishaps. Fear can be a good friend as long as it helps in physical survival. It keeps you away from dangers to life like unsafe driving or an exposure to risky environment. But in the form of worry it is more like an enemy that ruins the quality of life. Imagine the suffering that the thoughts of losing your reputation, wealth or a family member bring.

There are innumerable situations that create fear. A medical advice to get a biopsy performed to rule out a malignancy, the sight of a rope in the dark, an invitation to speak from the podium, can all generate fear. A good way to begin the process of accepting the fear is to pause and ask what is happening to you right in that moment. Address this enquiry to the sensation felt in your throat, heart or stomach. When we face fear by focusing on sensations, our mind immediately produces a story. It prompts us to plan a suitable response or lead you to assumptions, like – I am a failure, I am scared, people will soon find out and I will be thrown out. The key here is to move from imaginary mental stories to immediate contact with the sensations of fear – the squeezing, trembling and jittering. As you connect with the bodily sensations, the thoughts of fear begin to diminish. This leaning into fear can be terrifying, but if we let its sharp edges stab us or rip us initially something amazing happens. When there is no trying to control fear and clinging to life, we experience a deep sense of freedom. It offers an opportunity of letting go all that we cling to. Every day fears about our performance, financial condition or insecurity around our children can all be used to deepen the practice. Gradually we learn to handle our deepest fear – that of losing life.

We are born with an instinct to lean away from fear or push it away. But that does not help us in facing it the correct way. The solution lies in accepting the fear. Please remember that fear is only a form of energy – same as that of desire or anger. So turn around and face it directly, instead of resisting it. Facing means to feel the quivering, the shakiness or the gripping tightness that fear brings with it. The instinct to avoid all these sensations has to be overcome. This needs courage and commitment.

It is important to remember that there can be times when fear is too strong and there is a genuine difficulty to engage with it. In such situation it is advisable to seek professional help.

## 2.5 Accept your feelings

We have already discussed the meaning of accepting people, situations, ourselves, desires and fears. If you look at all these deeply, accepting these seemingly five different facets is, in one sense, nothing more than accepting certain feelings. Desire and fear are two different forms of feelings. Similarly, persons and situations also evoke feelings, which have to be dealt with. It will therefore, be useful to analyze 'feelings' in some details for better understanding.

A thought may have a feeling or a mix of feelings associated with it. Sometimes it is not easy to find whether a particular thought came first or the associated emotion. There are times we say, "I don't know why am I feeling so low" and at other times a thought flashes and feelings come tumbling out of nowhere. In either case, if we let the feeling pass, the thoughts will disappear too. To achieve this you will have to:

1. Become mindful of the feeling by watching it closely.
2. Let it come up as it arises. Just stay with it. Do not turn away. Let it run its course. Do not try to change or make it different from what it is.

This is relinquishing through pure awareness. Allow the feeling to rise at its own pace and intensity without resisting, venting, condemning or moralizing it. See it as a cloud of disturbed energy. Just be with the feeling as it is. Any effort to modify or resist the feeling in anyway will create conditions in which it will stay for a much longer time – maybe for rest of your life. Otherwise it will disappear as soon as the energy behind it dissipates. It is like a kite which keeps flying as long as the string holding it offers resistance to the wind which blows into it. No amount of wind can keep the kite in the air if the string snaps; it will come crashing down to the ground. When you cut the string of attachment or resistance, the kite of feelings, however high it may be flying, will fall back on the ground in no time.

Many times feelings are mixed. For example, the sight of father may evoke both hatred and fear in a child who is a victim of his abuse. Similarly, both guilt and shame can be experienced if you harm someone who had been helpful. In many situations if the resistance to the feelings is strong, facing the intensity of sensations becomes difficult. It is always useful to identify the mix of feelings and relinquish all of them. Thoughts are endless and self-reinforcing. They are used to rationalize those feelings. So it is important that we do not pay any attention to thoughts and instead only attend to the feelings. We should scan our body to clearly notice the sensations especially in the throat, chest, abdomen and stomach. Now inquire "What is happening? Why am I sad?" Pay close attention. This enquiry will awaken us to the experience of sadness exactly as it is in that moment. Sometimes, it is useful to name the feeling we have noted. For example, if there is anxiety before you are going to give a talk, pause and name the feeling that you detected. It may be, "Afraid-afraid, Tight-tight". Remember if you will ignore the feeling, it will carry itself into the talk. The quality of your delivery will be adversely affected.

## 3. How to practice Acceptance

Regrets (of the past), helplessness (of the present) or bleakness (of the future) have marred our lives at some point. A young woman who suffers domestic violence regrets her decision to get married. A family undergoing the trauma of nursing a terminally ill member feels a sense of hopelessness. Parents, whose son has become a drug addict, may feel as if they have lost everything. These are serious circumstances in which extreme reaction is not surprising. But even in ordinary situations, like someone accidentally breaking a piece of crockery, people can go into a hysterical overdrive.

In situations of emotional disturbance, we make efforts to somehow brush aside the unpleasantness. Some people might resort to excessive talking, or shopping or praying. Others may go numb and show symptoms of some illness or suffer a psychological breakdown. Such people are advised to chant mantras, read scriptures or pray. The reprieve is usually short but can be extended over longer periods if pursued with zeal. It helps in holding the mind in a position of minimum grief. But this delicate balance is invariably lost when the emotional storm gathers force.

Whatever may be the subject of acceptance (people, situation, things or ourselves) there is a common ground from which acceptance must be approached.

### 3.1 What is the common ground from which acceptance can be approached?

The answer is: "Taking a Pause."

This is not as easy as it sounds. The ability to simply pause and notice a sensation is actually rare. Unfortunately our teachers, preachers and elders have remained unaware of its power to change experience and consequently our lives. As a result no effort or time could be invested in educating the next generation in the art of taking pause. On the contrary much emphasis has been given to seek safe and secure environment. The evolutionary process and compulsions of living in social system has taught us to stay alert and vigilant about the likely threats. This is the fundamental reason of our tendency to control people, objects and events. To let go and take hands off the steering wheel of life is considered suicidal. Therefore, the science behind taking a break and the art of observing has not become a part of our up-bringing.

## How to take a Pause?

The term 'Pause' means suspension of activity. It is a time of temporary disengagement with the world. While taking a pause there should neither be any goal nor any internal exhortation like "what do I do next". It can be taken at anytime and may last for an instant or more. When you are doing something, say reading, working on a computer, cleaning, eating – pause for a moment or two. Just discontinue what you are doing. Let go of thinking and relax the body. Close your eyes and move awareness from toe to head scanning each limb of the body. Observe sensations, wherever they are experienced in the body.

You can also take a pause by taking time off and arranging an undisturbed space. Sit down with eyes closed. Reawaken attention to breath. Watch it come in and go out. Inhale-exhale-Inhale consciously for as long as possible. As you do this, attention will keep shifting from breath to random thoughts. As soon as you notice this, bring the attention back on your breath. Don't be disheartened if you keep failing. This is normal; keep perseverance.

People presume that taking a pause means going on a retreat or walking in nature or taking a sabbatical. This is not necessary. It is best practiced in routine, everyday life in the middle of whatever good or bad that is happening. You can pause during a conversation letting go of what you were about to say. Instead listen to and be with the other person. You can see breath enter and exit while travelling or attending a meeting or even while facing a challenging situation.

Treat pause as a sacred activity. You can weave it in your daily routine by choosing an activity – like bathing, making a phone call or turning your computer on. Take a pause immediately before this activity. It will bring the spirit of a fresh beginning in the most mundane affair.

Taking a pause is a very common practice in

Buddhist monasteries. A gong is struck at regular intervals as a signal for the monks to immediately disengage with whatever they are doing. They bring awareness back to their breath. By doing so, the mind comes back home back to the body. The monks do it all their life.

## 3.2 Love yourself to accept yourself

It is a universal truth that everyone is imperfect in his own unique way. A deep understanding of the fact that nobody is perfect brings a sense of relief and confidence. At the work place, in families, and in other relationships, we expect others to be perfect and scorn at their shortcomings. But our response to the imperfections of someone we deeply love is different. Their flaws are not easily visible and if they are noticed, we tend to justify them. "My mother is superstitious because she comes from a very orthodox family." "My son is getting difficult because of his nagging wife." Love, it seems, dilutes the intensity of faults. This implies that self-love can help us to come to terms with our own shortcomings. The acuteness of inadequacy gets softened and becomes a part of life without sticking out like a sore thumb.

However, some people think they are perfect. They have an enormous capacity to find faults with everyone (and everything), except themselves. Such people enjoy looking down upon others and also revel being looked up to. Are these arrogant self seeking individuals, who are full of themselves, also practicing self-love? Certainly not. Self-love and egotism are mutually exclusive. Anyone who has learnt to be in love with himself will neither seek approval nor be affected by criticism or refusal to admire him. He is free from dependence on others for endorsement. There is a realization that everyone is special by virtue of his strengths and weakness. This understanding helps in appreciating the uniqueness of others as well. Self-love allows you to be more loving in general and enhances acceptance of others. It dilutes the sense of identity and makes experience of oneness with others possible.

We offer care to others for various reasons. Visiting people in the midst of tragedies, sickness or difficulties is a common practice. Whatever be the reason, a hug or a sympathetic ear initiates a process of deep healing. The act of treating others with kindness is universally promoted. Physical, emotional and social support to those in crisis is ingrained deeply in our customs and cultures. But when it comes to the question of how we should treat ourselves, societies have adopted a different approach. Anyone paying attention to his own comforts and preference is labeled selfish. If you do not show signs of guilt or shame after committing a blunder you will be labeled shameless. We are expected to make sacrifices for the good of others. Society values people who take pains in helping others or show signs of deep remorse when their act is disapproved by the community. Also, a lot of time is wasted in making efforts to please others and wear garbs of goodness. Unfortunately, a large number of people live in unnecessary shame, guilt and low self-esteem. Some are so unforgiving when it comes to their own failures that they commit suicide.

We treat the rest of the world gently, but are unable to treat ourselves kindly. The idea of comforting ourselves with our own kind words may sound weird, out of place and embarrassing. Social work, charity, volunteering and donations are held in high esteem but paying enough attention to oneself is interpreted as an act of self indulgence – a trait that is deplored by societies. When a child cries, the mother knows it is time to cuddle him. When your heart cries, remember it is asking to be held in the compassionate embrace of a loving mother. The only way this motherly hug can happen is by self-loving; where you are the holder and also the held. You embrace yourself, share your own grief with yourself and caress your own back.

A mirror is a very effective tool in learning self-love. When something good happens in your life, you look into the mirror and say, "Thank you! Thank you for doing this." If something bad happens, you can go to the mirror and say, "This too shall pass. I love you and that's forever". It is not easy to face the mirror initially. But with time you become less self-critical. The words said in front of a mirror will sink to a deeper level.

It will take only a second to say, "Hello" or "Looking good" or "Cheer up. Isn't this fun?" before the mirror. You experience a deeper and enriching relationship with yourself if a mirror is used for complimenting, approving and supporting yourself. Many times we feel inadequate if criticized for a mistake at work or when accomplishments of others are extolled. It becomes easier to accept these situations if discussed openly before a mirror. The mirror can easily reflect your feelings and make you aware of what is being resisted. Once this resistance is clearly identified, it can be dropped.

Remember the spark in the eyes of your:

- mother when you received prize in school or
- school friend who met after a long time or
- beloved when you proposed marriage

Can you also look at yourself through those beautiful eyes? There is an interesting saying "God, help me to see myself the way my dog sees me." Every time a dog meets the master, it wags the tail. You should start wagging yours, every time you look in the mirror. Compliment yourself on all the small things accomplished. This will gradually build the capacity to accept situations in which you failed.

## 4. Acceptance and blockages

We learnt in Chapter 2-The Space Within (Part One) how the energy of stimulus which does not pass through seeks release through an emotional upsurge. If this rising is unpleasant, we instinctively avoid it; if it is pleasant, we instinctively hold it. By shoving it aside or clinging to this upsurge, the energy of disturbance gets trapped within the system. This stuck energy, which is like a small cloud of smoke that is unable to find a passage for escape, is called an 'impression'. It carries all details of thoughts, feelings and images related to an event and stays as such for decades. For example an 'impression' formed by a childhood abuse can, many years later, bring to surface the associated fear and insecurity. The euphoria of winning a keenly contested competition or making a discovery can also be relived any time in life. This happens because there is a corresponding 'impression' which can be stimulated. We add to the existing stock of impressions, simply by averting or adhering to an experience, on a daily basis without realizing the ramifications. Nature builds a protective shield around the 'impression' so that their contents do not pop up in awareness. Imagine countless impressions releasing details of experience stored in them at random. It will drive anyone insane. The shielded impressions, called 'fragments', continue to grow in numbers. They work as blockages obstructing the flow of energy through the heart thereby making us feel low. They are the seeds of suffering we sow every day.

However, in the case of a man who lives in acceptance the default response is different. Let us examine how. Genuine acceptance means that we know the event and the experience exactly the way 'it is'. There is no struggle either to overlook or justify it. This state is achieved only when movement of energy is neither resisted nor seized. The outside event, and also the ripples it created within, are fully felt and acknowledged. As a consequence, the awareness remains centered without getting trapped in the disturbance. When acceptance becomes the default response, energy passes through without any kind of obstruction. The formation of impressions is therefore becomes difficult. Thus the possibility of the heart getting clogged will be minimized.

Acceptance is thus a powerful tool that helps keep the heart open. As a navigator, it will always make you turn in the right direction.

# F FOR FORGIVENESS

## Chapter 8

# F For Forgiveness

The dictionary meaning of the word 'Forgiving' is:

*"To stop blaming or being angry with someone for something that person has done or not to punish them for something."*

Most of us understand forgiving as:

- stopping to hold others responsible for a particular happening, or
- not being angry anymore for something done by a person, or
- having decided not to chastise an offender

Unfortunately this does not convey the real meaning, power and significance of the word, 'forgiveness'. In its true sense, forgiving is not an act but a process of self healing which goes beyond physical and psychic boundaries. This chapter is an attempt to understand what forgiveness actually is, the profound impact it has on relationships, physical health, mental state and consequently, our capacity to live joyfully.

A thousand different things for example a rebuke, discourtesy, a threat or an assault can hurt us. It is impossible to prepare an exhaustive list because most of the time, context of the incident is more important than its content. In one situation, a fleeting glance and in another, a fixed gaze can be equally painful. It is common to hear people say, "Nobody paid attention to me." Or, "He stared through me." Much depends on how a situation is interpreted. Since each person perceives differently, therefore understanding and narration of an event will also be different from one person to another. However, irrespective of the way things are construed, everyone wants to eliminate the pain they create. There is a constant struggle that goes on with a grievance as we push it out of the conscious mind in an attempt to minimize the impact. All societies consider "Forgive and forget" as a valuable philosophy. It recommends a simple strategy (even though it is totally wrong): "do not keep in mind either the offender or the offense." This idea has been encouraged since times immemorial because it dilutes the urge of reprisal, at least in the short term. The possibility of starting a chain of conflicts is minimized, making it a useful tool of keeping peace in the society. In this context, it is not surprising to find that most cultures place forgiveness on a high moral plane. Almost all religious scriptures strongly endorse it. Alexander Pope wrote "To err is human and to forgive divine" three hundred years ago.

Forgiveness, when portrayed as a manifestation of divinity in men, becomes a decoration which makes an impressive display and bestows great social esteem. People are inspired, cajoled or even forced to play this game of showing off. A mind conditioned to 'forgive and forget' actually turns a blind eye to the situation – the demon becomes invisible but does not disappear for good. Burying the memory of the event (that caused hurt) in a space outside the conscious mind is an act of suppression. A casual observer may perceive it as a genuine and final truce. Such forgetting may minimize the interpersonal strife in the short-term but its impact on human psyche is, to say the least, tragic. Our inability to recognize this fact further compounds the tragedy.

This chapter offers an opportunity to scratch the surface to see the underlying truth. It seeks an authentic answer to the questions like "Can we really forgive by forgetting?" or "Whether forgiving is a passive act or an active process?" Some consider forgiveness to be a divine quality while others view it as refuge of the weak. The subscribers of these two opposite outlooks vehemently argue their respective cases. Such dispute is in fact proof of the prevailing ignorance about the profound nature of forgiveness.

Forgiving is a simple concept but widely misunderstood. Its meaning and also the implications of effecting it, as discussed in this chapter, may not be easy to comprehend. Therefore, it would be useful to drop all views, notions and thoughts we hold about forgiveness and start afresh.

Forgiveness can be understood in its true sense if we not only know what it means but also know what it does not mean.

**Forgiveness means that we:**

- take responsibility for the way we feel
- heal our hurt
- stop blaming others
- act like a hero and not a victim of a situation

**Forgiveness does not mean that we:**

- condone
- forget a painful happening
- overlook a misconduct
- adopt it as a virtue
- deny being hurt

- reconcile to a situation
- surrender to any other person
- ignore our feelings
- allow the offender go unpunished
- are weak

This description of 'what it means' and 'what it does not mean' is not commensurate with our traditional understanding of forgiveness. For example, to forgive and to pursue the case against an offender to get him punished sounds contradictory. Similarly, how can we forgive and yet not condone? Again what purpose is served by forgiving if we are not going to ignore our feelings about the offense or the offender? How can we stop blaming without surrendering to the person who caused the hurt? People become suspicious if told that they can forgive without bothering about what happens to the offender. These doubts are not easy to resolve.

It is not an overstatement that avenge is the foundation of our social, cultural and familial moorings. History is replete with stories of kings waging war because they were slighted. The pride that goes with such aggression makes for a powerful narration. By presenting affronts as threat to their nation, rulers can arouse the animal spirit in an otherwise civilized populace. This is eventually justified as nationalism of the highest order. There is almost a consensus that anyone who inflicts an injury, physical or psychological, should not go unpunished. In India, there are communities that carry hostilities over generations as a matter of obligation. The family insults are avenged in a most gruesome manner to make sure that they becomes a part of the folklore. Deeply ingrained social endorsement of such unfortunate acts of vengeance makes forgiving even more difficult. We do not need any formal training in learning to get angry, develop hatred, jealousy, or fear uncertainties; these come naturally. But forgiving does not happen on its own; it has to be learnt through deep understanding and committed practice.

It would be useful to address some common misgivings about forgiveness and also understand few related issues by answering the following questions:

**Q.1 How can we forgive those who commit heinous crimes like rape or murder?**

Forgiveness does not imply that any criminal act has to be condoned. No society can function if people are not made accountable for their wrongdoings. Therefore, a criminal must be prosecuted and sent to gallows if need be. Forgiving simply means that the psychic wound inflicted by the crime must be treated and cured.

**Q.2 Does forgiveness come in the way of seeking justice?**

This question is essentially similar to one asked above. To forgive does not mean to give up efforts for seeking justice or claiming compensation. To forgive is one thing and to punish the offender is another. Forgiveness does not expedite or delay trial. People think if the criminal is punished, it would be easier to come to terms with the crime. In other words healing will be easier if the wrongdoer is punished. The number of people who subscribe to this thinking is alarmingly high. But it is important to understand that there is no assurance of getting healed even if the wrongdoer is punished. We will understand the truth of this assertion later in this chapter.

**Q.3 Do we have to continue our relationship with people who have hurt us?**

Forgiving is all about letting go the grievances that we nurse. This process is about us and has nothing to do with anyone else. There is no need to have physical or psychological proximity with the offender as there is no dependence on him. The question of continuing or maintaining any relationship therefore, does not arise. This is why it is possible to forgive even the dead.

**Q.4 Why is forgiveness a better choice?**

In a given situation, a person may:

- Get angry for a short while
- Nurse a grudge for lifelong
- Simply let the problem slide off their backs
- Fail to cope and breakdown
- Feel compassionate
- Remain confused about what should be done
- Choose to forgive

Every person is differently conditioned and therefore his response to a given situation is also different. Even though forgiveness is available as a choice, it is not preferred since people consider it as refuge of the weak. By doing so, they miss the opportunity of using it to enhance the quality of their life.

The inspiration to forgive can also be drawn from the idea that it is wrong to hold others responsible for the pain we store within. That is something we do to our selves. Remember the story of Jhumroo packing his lunch every day and still blaming his wife for the bad menu (This is in fact the essence of 'responsibility' we discussed in chapter 6). If the mind-space is occupied by things that have gone wrong, then anger, sadness and unhappiness will dominate. Appreciation of the existing good becomes difficult because awareness is drawn in by the grudges we hoard. Attention remains focused on the past; consequently we miss loving relations that surround us in the present. It is like a man who remembers his days of poverty so intensely that he is unable to enjoy the riches he now possesses. This living in the past, unfortunately, is considered by most of us as a natural condition from which there is no escape. Forgiving means breaking away from the past and living more in the present.

**Q.5 Why is forgiveness rare, although men of eminence have always prescribed it?**

Consider the following quotes:

*The weak can never forgive. Forgiveness is the attribute of the strong.*
—Mahatma Gandhi

*The stupid neither forgive nor forget; the naive forgive and forget; the wise forgive but do not forget.*
—Thomas Szasz

*All major religious traditions carry basically the same message; that is love, compassion and forgiveness. The important thing is they should be part of our daily lives.*
—Dalai Lama

*Forgiveness liberates the victim. It's a gift you give yourself.*
—T. D. Jakes

These quotes make for a good conversation. But we do not become forgiving even though we have read them many times over. It cannot be denied that understanding their essence is important, but actual transformation is possible only when these words become a living experience. Therefore, forgiveness must be deeply practiced and not just understood intellectually. That is the only way forward.

**Q.6 Why do we get hurt?**

Every person has a unique mental frame built by his personal experiences and perceptions. For example, you may prefer tea without sugar, but your father might like two spoonfuls. Or you might think studying regularly is essential, but your teenage son may have a different theory about learning. He prefers to pick up his books immediately before the examinations are to commence. Or you can be passionately socialist and your colleague may think free market is the best solution. So you may ask for sugarless tea, regular studies and a socialist government. But your father, son and colleague differ. This does not matter but the problem starts when you

- Want your father to stop taking sugar
- Force your son to study everyday
- Protest if the government allows free market

Now the otherwise innocuous preferences become

prescriptions for others. It is imposing "my rules" on them. Why do you want to enforce your preferences? Why should people comply with your rules? Are they not free to exercise their choices? Look at the following 'should' statements:

- One should be faithful
- People should speak the truth
- Life should be fair
- People should treat others with kindness
- Parents should not send children to boarding schools
- We should be honest

All values are basically in the nature of expectations. That is why efforts to force or inspire people to fulfill them does not succeed. Men continue to defy them and, hence, there is no dearth of unfaithful, unfair, callous and dishonest people. The inevitability of this situation, if recognized, will help in appreciating a basic fact – people are free to make choices and behave accordingly. They will not change because somebody wants them to. Would you change because the neighbor wants you to? You might think that if people comply with your set of rules, the world would be a better place. Yes it would be, but only for you. We invite grievance by insisting on compliance with a set of rules which are preferred by us. Who is responsible for the consequent suffering when people refuse to do so? Ponder over it and find your answer.

Incidentally we are not arguing against prescribing values or enforcing a code of ethical conduct or administering a legal system. The only point is to know the inherent flaw in wanting others to meet our expectations and not to get stressed when that does not happen.

## Grievance– The root of all pain

Ultimately, forgiving means to heal our hurt. This, in other words, amounts to dissolving the grievances – the root of all pains.

A grievance starts building up when:

i. something we did not want, happens, or something we wanted does not happen; and

ii. we do not accept what has happened

There are three stages of this build-up:

i. The offense caused by an event is taken personally

ii. The person responsible for the offense is clearly identified and blamed

iii. A narrative is created.

Let us examine these stages in some detail.

Stage 1: The offense caused by an event is taken personally

Suppose a colleague narrates the insulting treatment meted out to him at the workplace. You can console him or suggest how to seek justice or overcome the trauma. Even though you may be genuinely sympathetic, you are unlikely to experience the intensity of pain that he suffered. When you are not personally involved in any incident, the grievance does not build up. Personal involvement does not mean that you have to be directly affected by the incident. The nature of the incident and your relationship with the person who was hurt determines whether a grievance will arise or not. For example, parents can be deeply affected if their child is hurt, even though they are not part of the incident.

Every incident has two parts – a personal side and an impersonal side. For example, getting angry on discovering that you have been duped is the personal part. But when you find that the same man cheated half the neighborhood, a sense of relief descends. This is the impersonal part. Similarly, people find it very difficult to come to terms with a sudden diagnosis of a serious medical condition. An overwhelming sense of disbelief descends as they protest "Oh! God, Why me?" Over time, this complaining can diminish considerably when they meet and share experiences with other people suffering similar disease. This identification with others is also the impersonal part of the grievance.

It is easy to find the personal part but the impersonal part in any situation cannot be easily detected. Children nurse grudges against their parents for not loving them enough. But later in life, when they discover that their parents had been beset with marital discord or financial stress or had lived in fear of adversaries, the grievances against the parents may start dissolving. Similarly, a man convicted for a gruesome murder may earn public sympathy (and, maybe even reprieved) if it was found that his criminal act was caused by a tumor in the brain. Suddenly, the whole picture changes and the intensity of social outrage waters down. Our response changes when certain aspects of a situation, hitherto unknown, come to light. This allows us to see a particular situation from a very different perspective. This is what constitutes the impersonal dimension.

Stage 2: The person responsible for hurt is clearly identified and blamed

This is the beginning of the second step in the grievance process – the blame game. It is easy to identify the person responsible for our suffering. We gather evidence (and sometimes even fabricate it) to prove our point against him. Blaming basically means that someone else is the cause. It creates a good versus bad narrative. Most of the time whether the other person really intended to hurt is not even considered. All that matters is the way a situation is perceived.

Stage 3: A narrative is created

The narrative about the grievance is the story that the victim tells about the incident in question. The script of the story assigns meaning to the incident and it accordingly etches itself in the psyche of the listener. Usually in such narrative bitterness occupies centre stage. The way this story is created, narrated and recounted determines the extent to which the narrator is hurt.

In practice, a story should be just good enough to convey an overview of what happened. For example, while describing a recent vacation, we name the destination, list our reasons for choosing it, mention the places visited and major hiccups if any. Nobody recounts a minute to minute description of the event (a vacation in this case). Each actor in a story – the villain, the witness, the cohort or the victim – describes the event in his own way. Everyone has a different view point and hence a unique description. This plurality of views is inevitable in light of the fact that the psyche of every individual is distinctive. Each narration leaves out or highlights some part and interprets or misinterprets some other. It is not possible to include every standpoint in a singular narration. Each version is true in its own sense although it is not easy to say which is more reliable than the other.

The nature and depth of a grievance determines the way the victim chooses to write the final story. It is the script of the story which determines the gravity of the grievance.

## The unfolding of Forgiveness

Forgiving, simply stated, means self-healing. It unfolds according to its own natural process. The fact that:

- A hurt exists, and
- Something needs to be done to heal it

must first be accepted before we start practicing forgiveness. The following questions should be clearly answered:

- When was the hurt first felt?
- What actions actually caused that hurt?
- Did you share it with someone you trust?

The answer to the first question demands that you should clearly know the feeling of hurt when it occurred. It may not be simple because feelings come in mixture of two or more. For example they can manifest in twos – upset and confused, furious and abandoned, alone and scared. Also the feelings may linger for a long time or disappear quickly.

The second question demands that you know the exact action (whether verbal, physical, psychological, direct or indirect) which is at the root of the grievance. This means trying to remember it in as much detail as possible. But it is important that the incident should not, in any way whatsoever, be denied or minimized.

The third question hints at the importance of sharing the incident with trusted people. Words lend clarity to expressed feelings and allow others to offer care, guidance and support. If no one is available, write down the experience on paper and review it. It can be shared anonymously in chats on the internet, but never with people you do not trust. Please remember that to talk openly with one or two persons is different from talking about it with twenty people. Usually, a story is shared with many only to ensure wider censure of the offender. It is a cry of pain meant to inform people that we have been victimized. This is amplifying and not sharing.

Forgiveness does not happen by following any rigorous schedule of suggested activities. Nor does it follow any timelines. No single pace is right for everyone. It can neither be forced nor does it happen by accident. Sometimes only an intention or a decision to forgive is enough, and at other times it may take long and yet not help fully. To some it might look like the beginning of a new chapter rather than the end of an ongoing story.

Forgiving is not our default response because we are conditioned to blame others. Therefore, it is a difficult choice to make because the reasons for not doing so appear very logical and appealing. People may think that a particular incident was too grave to qualify for forgiveness. Others might feel guilty if they do not avenge a wrongdoing – for them family honor comes first. Forgiveness becomes even more difficult if the associated emotional currents become stronger. It is obvious from the questions answered in this chapter, that there are several mental blocks to forgiving.

We think that ordinarily people are not willing to forgive. This is not a fact but a figment of widely accepted imagination. There is no doubt that everyone, whether a friend or a foe, wants peace of mind. But is it possible unless they let go their grievances? So anyone wanting this peace actually wants to heal his hurts. In that sense, it is nothing but a desire to forgive. People do not recognize that they actually yearn to forgive.

## Methods of forgiving

Although our upbringing, education, social values, religious beliefs and traditional wisdom emphasizes on the virtue of forgiving but they do not offer methods that help us bring it to effect. The failure of civilized society to devise effective ways of forgiving has caused immense suffering to people – something which could have been avoided.

Broadly there are two techniques of forgiving:

(i) To bear the pain that the incident brought on

(ii) Developing new mental patterns

**(i) To bear the pain that the incident brought on**

In this method, you recall the incident clearly identifying the actions that you believe brought about the pain. As you go back in the memory lane, the feelings related to that particular incident will start appearing. Allow the story of the grievance to play. Sit back and experience the feelings without modifying them in any way. Do not resist anything. Your mind would desperately want to shift to other thoughts so as to avoid the pain. As soon as you realize this, go back to the incident.

This process will crack open the 'fragment' which was created by the incident in question. The details of the incident and related feelings, which are contained therein in the form of trapped energy, will be released. By repeating this exercise many times over, the grievance begins to dissolve and pain gradually diminishes. This is one way of healing the wound.

The narrative of grievance loses its force, and blaming recedes. The stuck energy of the impression begins to pass through and the healing starts. Forgiveness is full and final when the hurt is completely healed. In this process neither the wrongdoer is punished nor is the memory of the incident in question erased. Also the offender is not doing anything to assuage your pain. In fact, there is no positive act that can be called, "act of forgiving". It is the outcome of a process that heals the psyche.

When people say that time is a great healer, they are unknowingly talking about this process of relieving the pain by reliving it. Time, by itself, does not heal. The fact is that as people go back to their grievance repeatedly over a period of time, they keep contacting the pain again and again. Over time, the energy of the pain abates. In other words forgiving begins to take roots. Forgiveness will not change the past but it transforms the way it feels in the present.

### (ii) Developing new mental patterns

Our opinions, presumptions and expectations create mental patterns which govern our response to worldly stimuli. They are deeply ingrained in us and therefore, rigorous discipline is required to erase or redraw some.

The following exercises help in developing new mental patterns and also demonstrate their impact:

(a) Filling Yourself with the Positive

In our daily life, happiness is short-lived whereas hurts stay for a much longer duration and look more real. In other words, happiness is fleeting whereas sorrow lingers on. Past incidents continue to upset us in the present. For example, it is difficult to forget the betrayal of a trusted friend. Even after years, the memory of the treachery stings. Now, compare it with an event like meeting an old friend or the scenic beauty of a sunset you witnessed on a beach. It is difficult to recall and hold back those joyous moments for long. This is because we give more mental space to negativities like fear, worry, resentment and guilt. We discussed the strong evolutionary reasons for this in chapter 7.

To change this state, more mind-space should be made available for things like the love of family or beauty of a mountain stream or a stunning rainbow after rains. The emphasis on positive experiences must increase. It will reduce the habit of dwelling on grievances and therefore alleviate the suffering. This is quite similar to switching TV channels. If your mind is tuned into the grievance channel, make a conscious effort and switch to the gratitude channel. This requires a degree of awareness which is made possible by the practice of "Pause". How long do you wish to watch a particular channel is a personal choice. Make effort to recall the moments of joy experienced in the past and stay with them for as long as possible. It could be the warm embrace of your mother, the strong support of your father or the tearful eyes of your beloved. We must consciously offer more space to things which give us joy. This is called filling oneself with positive experiences which will push grievances into a corner. This method offers symptomatic relief but does not cure the root cause of the problem. If you wish to redress the grievance, 'meeting the pain' is the only remedy.

Try doing the following:

- Stop for a while in front of a hospital and feel thankful that you are not in the ICU
- List as many persons as you can, who contribute to bringing food on your table, and thank them
- Watch your mind chatter when stuck in traffic
- Observe the innocence in the smile of a child
- Think of a moment you hurt someone, and seek forgiveness
- Remember when your mother blessed you
- Remember loving your child

These are some possible starting points but you must make your own list.

## Seeking forgiveness

There are many situations in which we blame others. Many times, these 'others' are not aware of this blaming and may even be unaware of having caused you a hurt. They might be surprised to hear your version of the story. Let us not forget that 'others' may also be blaming us for many things we are not aware of. We are quick to justify our actions and always believe they were inspired by good and authentic reasons. This refusal to take blame is not due to any dishonest intentions. It happens because the victim and the alleged offender perceive the same event differently. Both parties believe they are doing the right thing. Is it not paradoxical that in a world where everybody is doing right, there are so many disgruntled, frustrated and unhappy people? Obviously, something is fundamentally wrong.

The fact is that, knowingly or unknowingly, we hurt each other and there is no way to assess our contribution to the stock of pain in the world. It is therefore important that besides forgiving others, we seek their forgiveness too. This can be done in the following ways:

1. Sit comfortably in a quiet place. If you remember a specific incident that may have made someone unhappy, ask for forgiveness. You may have rebuked your subordinate in the office even though rightfully, in order

to maintain discipline. But it must have hurt him. He needs your apology. Close your eyes and remember that particular person and ask him to forgive you. You can say these words silently (i.e. without verbalizing): "I seek your kind favor. Please forgive me." It will not mean anything if it is done as a thought process. You should be filled with a deep sense of authentic apology. Repeat it as many times as you feel like. Do not visit him in person or even speak to him about this. This would be misunderstood and complicate the situation. Seeking forgiveness in person is not necessary.

2. Sit in a quiet corner. Make a small prayer by thanking natural forces (call it God, Almighty or whatever you prefer) for everything happening in life. Now write a letter to the person you wish to seek forgiveness from expressing apology for whatever happened. Don't be miserly in using words. Let details fill up the page. If you are short and cryptic the effect will be lost. Letter writing is helpful only if you allow your heart to melt and be poured out completely. Read it carefully – more than once if you feel like. Wait in silence for at least five minutes. Quietly shred the paper and throw it in the bin.

3. Before you go to sleep every night, sit

comfortably on the bed and close your eyes for a minute. At times we are unable to remember people we may have hurt. Therefore, it is a good practice to seek forgiveness from everyone at the end of the day.

If you have included these activities in your routine "to do list" remember there is no value in mechanical repetition. It must come from the core of your heart.

## Forgiving yourself

The four stages of the process by which we forgive others are:

i. An unwanted event causes a hurt,

ii. There is an intention to forgive,

iii. The pain is relieved through reliving it, and

iv. The hurt is healed.

This is easy to comprehend when the offender (who caused the hurt) and the offended (one who was hurt) are two distinct entities. There is a subject – object relationship between them. But the idea of hurting ourselves and therefore the need to heal ourselves is foreign to most of us. Let us see how it happens:

1. Suppose you stole money, or

2. Cheated your friend, or
3. Exploited someone misusing your position

Each of these situations can stimulate a unique feeling. In these three cases it could be guilt, shame and regret respectively. You feel low, repent having done it and may even want to undo the whole situation. No one is blaming you for stealing, cheating or exploiting. It is your private affair but you still find it difficult to cope with what you have done. The past may haunt and upset you repeatedly. There may be times in your life when you say, "Oh! God, why did I do it?" or express doubt "Was that the right thing to do?" All this suffering is arising because you have hurt yourself. This is an occasion to forgive yourself.

## How to forgive yourself?

The tools of forgiving yourself are the same as those meant for forgiving others. The most effective method is meeting the pain head on. It means recalling the thought that is troubling you, without resisting it in any way. The event has to be accepted in its totality. Do not try to justify it by saying, "I could not resist doing that," or "After all, there were reasons for my doing it." That is not going to help. Look for the pain that comes with recalling. Let the sting of committing a wrong arise. Just hold yourself with compassion, just like you embrace a grieving friend.

## The importance of forgiving

Forgiving is important not because it will reduce strife in society or is valued by a religious order. It is important because the accumulation of grievances within us impacts our biology severely and ultimately becomes the root cause of numerous physical and psychological ailments. So, forgiving (which is essentially a process of dissolving a grievance) also means choosing a healthier lifestyle. Let us investigate the truth of this assertion.

In case of physical attack, the body activates the flight, fight or freeze (3F) response. Flight or fight are stress responses that helps us to react on perceiving a threat. Freeze means to keep the movement on hold and ready oneself for the next move. It is reactive or attentive immobility. This is the basic instinct of survival, which is involuntary and an evolutionary human trait. But as man moved out of jungles, gave up nomadic life to settle down in a civilized society and equipped himself with ever advancing technology, the threat to his physical survival reduced. But the vulnerability in the psychological domain increased manifold. Situations like loss of prestige, humiliation, disrespect, worrying about an uncertain future and fear of losing accumulated wealth begun to be perceived as threats which could actuate 3F response. The affected person will either begin to fight the cause of hurt (say a person) or take the flight by moving away from the person (who caused the hurt) or freeze at physical and psychological level.

A situation which creates corporeal threat (example: road rage) or psychological threat (example: an abusive boss) are both interpreted as a threat to safety. The biological system prepares the body to either escape or fight by releasing certain hormones. This increases the heart beat, constricts the blood vessels and as a result the blood pressure rises. Breathing becomes shallower and senses are heightened so that the undisclosed threat, if any, can be detected. Digestion ceases and blood flow is diverted to the centre of the body making you feel jumpy and uncomfortable. The electrical activity in certain parts of the brain is reduced, making straight thinking difficult. In short, the entire biochemistry changes.

The 3F response is an instinct and not the outcome of any carefully conceived plan of response. It is understandable if it is brought into play when a physical threat is imminent. But unfortunately it is not limited to situations endangering the body. When psychological pain is caused by a real time event or on recalling an old memory, the biological system kick starts flight or fight mechanism in both cases. The human nervous system cannot distinguish between an old or a current psychological threat which appears in awareness. As a consequence, stress chemicals are produced internally. This process is invisible, involuntary and silent. By blaming and narrating grievance stories, we are actually releasing drugs that harm our system. Nursing a grievance therefore means taking slow poison. This condition is similar to the one created by an addict who destroys his health by injecting himself with narcotics. Rarely do people see this similarity.

## Forgiveness and Blockages

We learnt in Chapter 2-The Space Within (Part One) how the energy of stimulus which does not pass through seeks release through an emotional upsurge. If this rising is unpleasant, we instinctively avoid it; if it is pleasant, we instinctively hold it. By shoving it aside or clinging to this upsurge, the energy of disturbance gets trapped within the system. This stuck energy, which is like a small cloud of smoke that is unable to find a passage for escape, is called an 'impression'. It carries all details of thoughts, feelings and images related to an event and stays as such for decades. For example an 'impression' formed by a childhood abuse can, many years later, bring to surface the associated fear and insecurity. The euphoria of winning a keenly contested competition or making a discovery can also be relived any time in life. This happens because there is a corresponding 'impression' which can be stimulated. We add to the existing stock of impressions, simply by averting or adhering to an experience, on a daily basis without realizing the ramifications. Nature builds a protective shield around the 'impression' so that their contents do not pop up in awareness. Imagine countless impressions releasing details of experience stored in them at random. It will drive anyone insane. The shielded impressions, called 'fragments', continue to grow in numbers. They work as blockages obstructing the flow of energy through the heart thereby making us feel low. They are the seeds of suffering we sow every day.

But in case of a man who is forgiving the default response will be different. Let us examine how.

The occasion to forgive arises when you are hurt by some act of omission or commission. Now, a forgiving man knows that to heal the hurt the corresponding fragment must be exposed to the light of awareness. When he lets that happen, the fragment cracks open, bringing back a flood of pain. With the passage of time the trapped energy of the event in question (which caused the hurt in the first place) will pass through. The ache will stop. A forgiving person therefore, becomes skilled at dissolving old blockages. His heart will start unclogging, and therefore opening up. As the practice deepens, the need to consciously meet the pain will also be considerably reduced. This happens because the default response of a forgiving man is to let go. As soon as he feels the tinge of the hurt, his forgiving disposition withdraws resistance, if any, to the ripple of disturbance within. The energy will, therefore, pass through without creating a new impression. Therefore spawning of new fragments will also reduce.

Forgiving is thus a powerful tool for keeping the heart open. This allows the energy within to flow freely-essentially making us joyful. As a navigator Forgiveness will, therefore, always make you turn in the right direction.

# ALL IN ONE AND BEYOND

## Chapter 9

# All In One And Beyond

There is no dearth of people willing to offer advice on how to live happily – even though their personal stories do not make a good example of joyful living. However the popularity of some of these characters matches that of rock stars. They appear to be well versed in scriptures; some present themselves as mystically empowered and even proficient at solving mundane problems of the people. The presence of the rich, famous, highly placed and also common men in their durbars is offered and accepted as a proof of the powers attributed to them. They fill hearts of the thronging crowds with the hope that their wishes would be fulfilled and suffering purged. Despite all interventions by these 'Masters' it is still rare to find truly joyful persons. People swing between the fleeting happiness on one end and enduring pain on the other. The preponderance of suffering all around, despite variety of cures offered, indicates that something fundamental is being ignored.

Anyone interested in the subject of joyful living must know that there are no readymade 'off the shelf' solutions to fulfill this aspiration. The impermanent nature of everything in existence means that life situations will continue to change. That is beyond control. No amount of desperation to retain the good and spurn the bad will work. Also wisdom and understanding necessary for living in joy demands lot of unlearning. We need to know how we sow seeds of sorrow and harvest crops of pain. This is possible only when we stop looking outside for remedies and start looking within. GRAF and the techniques mentioned in this book offer methodology of taking this U-turn. The recognition 'what we seek, we already keep' occurs when this inner space is explored. We learn that joy is not manufactured or invented – it is a treasure to be discovered.

The power of **GRAF** can be summarized as under:

If you are **G**rateful, you are not resentful

If you are **R**esponsible, you are not hostile

If you **A**ccept, your response is correct

If you **F**orgive fully, you are holy.

This makes GRAF one of the most effective navigational tool for 'Making You Turn' on the right course – one that leads to the door of proverbial 'eternal spring of joy within' and unlocks it as well. To use this tool in daily life, we need a higher degree of awareness, patience and unwavering commitment. It is always a work in progress. The deeply etched old patterns of thinking persistently dissuade us from doing the work necessary to make GRAF a living experience. Because of these patterns, even the simple exercises described in chapter 10 become difficult. For the same reason even though gratitude, forgiveness and acceptance are considered founding stones of a spiritual life by many scriptures, yet people have not benefitted by the preaching. The solution to the pain we carry cannot be found in anything outside-it has to come from within.

To be able to look inside we need both courage and conviction – something not easy to obtain. Even the most common and seemingly simple exercise of looking within – focusing attention on breath – is not easy. As you watch it enter and leave the body, the attention quickly moves from one thought to another. As soon as you become aware of this distraction, you bring attention back to the breath. This exercise tethers the mind to the present – the only place where we are truly alone and still. The deeper experience involved in this process is described by Greek monk Maximos Constas as under:

*"If I can get my mind to focus on the breath I'm not only entering into my body but I'm also entering into the present. It is so tremendously powerful to be in the*

*present. It can be frightening because it's a place we're not familiar with, and I think that's one of the reasons we run from it. It can be overwhelming."*

This description hints at the enormous challenge that a simple breathing exercise throws up in our effort to look within.

Our deeply conditioned mind questions the rationale of living in GRAF. For example read the following widely accepted viewpoints:

- Some people are extremely annoying
- Forgiving is the attribute of the weak
- Anyone who is happy with what he already has will cease to be ambitious
- Do not accept things you do not like

All these ideas look absolute truths in such an obvious way that we do not seek evidence to prove them. That is why we do not question them and allow them to occupy a large part of our mind-space. The possibility of experiencing the profound through GRAF is lost when we fall prey to the trappings of such statements.

To a casual observer, Gratitude, Responsibility, Acceptance and Forgiveness appear as four distinct entities. Let us examine if it is actually so. We discussed earlier that a truly grateful man can easily see the abundance. The understanding that he is already bestowed with innumerable gifts greatly reduces the feeling of lacking in life. A man with a grateful disposition, therefore, does not get disturbed or overwhelmed when unwanted things happen. Since his awareness is focused on the existing good, therefore it does not easily get drawn into the feeling of inadequacy. For him, an undesirable situation is one off amongst plenty of good ones. He acknowledges the plenty which the universe has bestowed, absolutely unencumbered, to him. This state of being weakens the tendency to resist, avoid or deny the unwanted. The situation can therefore be seen as 'it is' with a clear mind. This mental composure is nothing but 'acceptance' of the situation. This means that **Gratitude brings Acceptance in life.**

Ordinarily, people brush aside hurts and buries them in the deeper recesses of their mind. They carry on with the business of life, apparently unaffected. But this suppression does not redress the grievance. So, the wound within continues to fester. If any efficacious cure has to be found, the sensation of hurt must first be closely examined. Obviously, pushing it under the carpet will be counterproductive. To genuinely analyze, it would be essential to experience the hurt as it is, without modifying in any manner whatsoever. This is the condition that is precedent for effective healing and it demands that we clearly identify the act which caused the hurt. To know this, we will have to see it through the lens of an undisturbed mind. This is possible only when the incident is accepted in the first place. Healing starts only after such acceptance happens. This healing, we know is forgiving. This means that **Acceptance takes us to the doorsteps of Forgiveness.**

We carry innumerable grievances in our hearts. As we discussed in earlier chapters – they create blockages eventually reducing the flow of energy. An old blockage begins to dissolve when forgiving heals the corresponding hurt. The associated pain gradually disappears. As the practice of forgiveness deepens, time taken to heal the hurt is considerably reduced. This implies that the person would stop carrying the grievance for long. The time gap between the occurrence of the incident and the healing of the hurt it caused becomes increasingly small. Experientially it means that the world outside will stop hurting the men of forgiving disposition in any manner whatsoever. In other words, these men become masters of their inner world. The outside can no more decide the state of their inside. This is the typical characteristic of responsible men. This means that **Forgiving makes a man Responsible.**

Non-acceptance implies that we allow the external stimuli to become the centre of our attention. Such, mind remains turbulent because it will constantly engage in complaining and comparing. Restoration of peace within becomes impossible. In other words, the world outside begins to exercise control on the way we feel and behave. Clearly, non-acceptance makes a man irresponsible. The simple corollary would be that **Acceptance makes a man Responsible.**

Clearly G leads to A, A leads to F, F leads to R. So, if you start with the practice of gratitude, sooner or later the other three aspects would also manifest.

The organic link, between them is indeed strong. For example, if you have learnt to accept, forgiveness will become easy. Forgiving will heal hurts, which makes you responsible. This in turn, will bring a deep sense of acceptance. This makes the mind so calm and clear that bounties of nature and gifts of grace become clearly visible. An overpowering feeling of thankfulness starts arising. This is gratitude. So anyone who learns the skill of acceptance becomes forgiving. This makes him responsible and grateful, too. It is like strings of a musical instrument which are tuned in such a way that when one is plucked, the other three resonate. Some people find it easy to start from gratitude whereas others prefer forgiveness. It varies from one person to another. Therefore, pick that constituent of GRAF which naturally connects with you.

Work with absolute commitment to make it an

integral part of your existence, like your heartbeat or blood circulation.

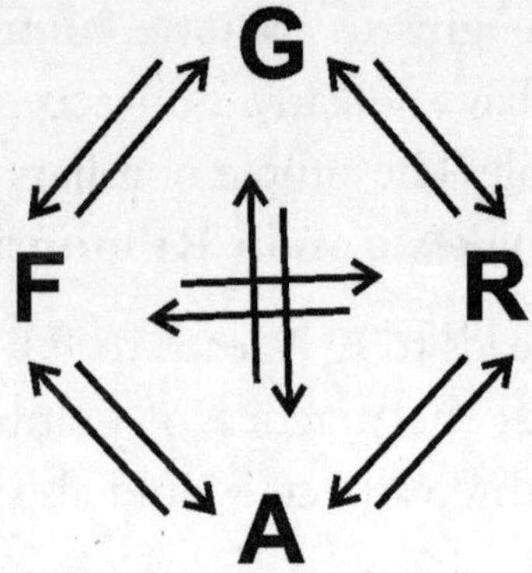


This image shows that we can reach any point irrespective of where we start from. Nobody can advise what is best for you. Follow the path that comes naturally to you. All four constituents of GRAF coexist; always inseparable from each other. They are not standalone entities but come in one single package – All in One.

We have described in earlier chapters that gratitude, responsibility, acceptance and forgiveness are fundamental tools of dissolving blockages in the heart. They keep the heart open so that the flow of energy inside remains uninhibited. This, we said earlier, is the key to joyful living. Gratitude, Responsibility, Acceptance and Forgiveness as simple words of language do not convey the enormity of their transformational capacity; the key lies in practicing them. They have to be experienced and not just studied as subjects of an academic discourse. Is there any choice except to step into a pool to know and experience swimming? The knowledge of the Archimedes principle does not help you float; only practice does. Similarly all claims about the power of GRAF to bring a new high of tranquility never felt before is hollow unless personally experienced. Scholarly discussions do not change conditioning of the mind and patterns of thinking – only practice of correct techniques makes it possible.

That brings us to another fundamental question: is mitigation of suffering, which comes with the practice of GRAF, an end in itself or is there anything beyond it? Nevertheless, to peep into what lies beyond, let us first recapitulate the significance of GRAF:

1. Gratitude dissolves the sense of entitlement and allows us to see everything as a gift of nature. It brings humility and a sense of abundance. The compassionate embrace of the universe becomes visible.

2. A responsible man understands that he is the master of the world within, therefore, he stops blaming others for causing hurt by an act of commission or omission. His emotional state depends solely on him and nobody else. There is no dependence on people for either joy or sorrow. He makes his own choice.

3. Acceptance is recognition of 'what is'. There is neither any denying nor avoiding without manipulating the event or a situation. All the pain or pleasure it brings is felt in totality. There is no resistance offered to an external event irrespective of the disturbance it can potentially cause. The reflexive resistance, otherwise caused by conditioning is surrendered as awareness comes into full play. Acceptance is not a passive non-action but a precondition necessary before action to mitigate a situation is taken.
4. Forgiveness, simply stated, is a process of self healing. It does not mean forgetting and letting the offender go unpunished. Very often people think they can forgive by simply stating so. Saying "I forgive you" does not mean anything. Forgiving happens when the hurt caused by the other person is healed. It does not require that the forgiver and the forgiven meet or engage in any direct conversation. Expressing regret or seeking pardon verbally or agreeing to condone the offence are not a part of this process.

GRAF empowers us to face both joy and sorrow with a deep sense of equanimity. We learn the art of responding according to the demands of a situation without getting overwhelmed. It unclogs the heart centre – the storehouse of emotions – by clearing the debris of residual remains of life experiences. The thoughts generated by the mind keep stoking emotions in the heart. For example the thought of being alone in old age may spawn fear. The emotions of the lower order (especially those mentioned at serial number 6 to 13 in the following paragraph) disturbs the heart which in turn disturbs the mind – in fact they begin to feed on each other causing untold misery. But when the awareness breaks free from the strangle hold of inner disturbances, the heart gradually relaxes and opens up. This joyful heart makes for a peaceful mind.

People spend all their time living in mind. They think about past events and future uncertainties, argue, conceive ideas, express views and engage themselves in many such intellectual activities. But the essence of life is not thoughts; it is the way you feel. The emotions that dominate our life are as under:

1. Bliss
2. Joy
3. Love
4. Peace
5. Trust
6. Pride
7. Anger

8. Desire
9. Fear
10. Grief
11. Despair
12. Guilt
13. Shame

Everything that each one of us does is primarily meant to bring joy and peace. They are feelings and not thoughts. Emotions at serial number 6 to 13 affect relationships, physical and emotional health adversely. People in these emotional states will create poor life conditions for themselves and also for others. They drain the energy of those coming in their contact. As the blockages start clearing through the practice of GRAF, we start moving up the ladder. The increased current of energy allows efficacious use of awareness to further purge the emotional debris which in turn further enhances the flow. A self-perpetuating process is thus set into motion.

It is equally important to understand that when awareness is drawn in by the movement of energy producing pleasant feelings, there is no resistance to the energy. Instead, there is reflexive holding which creates 'impressions' as well. This will force you to hold people, things and situations, which caused the clinging, close to your chest. You will want all of them to continue providing the comfort and happiness which they initially did. Out of this wanting our so called 'attachments' are born. These are the seeds of suffering that we sow. Little do we realize that everything in nature is transitory. It is impossible to maintain a status quo in respect of anything let alone the good feelings. Everything is destined to change whether you resist or cling to it. In both cases, we end up creating impressions which ultimately clog passage of energy. Therefore if we wish to stay centered, it is essential to let both go.

It is the capacity of the mind to think that has made all the growth and development possible. However, apart from this positive contribution, it also creates misery by engaging in relentless inner chattering. Therefore, the mind must be kept on a tight leash – making it work like a good servant and not allowing it to be a dominating master. Complaining (he did this to me), Criticizing (he is doing the wrong thing) and Comparing (I am better than him) dominates our thinking. If this stops, the mind can achieve a state of stillness. GRAF transforms our mind in way that brings an end to all our complaining, criticizing and comparing. You cannot be grateful and resentful at the same time. Every individual is distinct and cannot be expected to match the uniqueness of others. We also want people to do certain things in certain ways. In other words, we want to impose our rules on them leading to a lot of unrest. So comparing and criticizing ends with acceptance. By assuming responsibility, we stop getting affected when others fail to meet our expectations. GRAF, therefore, makes it possible for us to live in a space where there are no grudges, grievances and grumblings. The awareness remains centered allowing us to pay undistracted attention to anything we choose – be it the breath or the flow of thoughts or rising of any sensation in the body or the heart. Now we can see things as they are and not as they appear to us through the lens of conditioning. It is only an experience and not an experience of a thing. This is a state of being, unadulterated by thoughts and emotions, that transcend the mind. The door to another level of consciousness is unlocked – beyond the body, mind and heart.

We have been generally stating so far that thoughts evoke emotions. But is it really true that the emotions are always rooted in our thoughts? The answer is not always. For all practical purposes, in our daily life the role of thoughts in causing shifts of energy in the heart cannot be denied. How can you have anger, guilt or pride without a cause – which means there must be corresponding causal data stored in our memory. However, the emotions of higher order like unconditional love, joy and bliss are experienced only when we transcend mind. That means entering a realm beyond thoughts and hence the question of the corresponding emotional state being rooted in them does not arise. You cannot reach the higher levels of the ladder of emotions (see pp. 225 & 226) unless thoughts start thinning out. These levels are meditative states that create pleasant bodily sensations experienced as emotions of the higher order.

The question "What lies beyond GRAF?" is inspired by the desire to know what happens when someone begins to live GRAF in the right earnest. The answer is simple – thoughts thin out and the heart marinates in peace. Some schools of spiritual pursuits call this a space of no thought or absolute silence, our 'true nature'. GRAF therefore enables us to access the space which defines who we truly are or where we exist in our true nature. In that sense it holds promise of self-realization. This is the space that we yearn returning to – the real homecoming. This domain by definition is beyond mind and therefore cannot be reduced to a concept for meaningful intellectual debate. Transcending the mind implies going beyond the realm of intellect and entering a deep meditative state. Lao Tzu in his work Tao Te Ching said "Those who know do not speak and those who speak do not know." The difficulty in describing the experience of this space must have been the reason why most realized sages chose to remain reticent. Perhaps they felt that narration would debase something very profound. So, they preferred silence. The reticence of those who experienced it is, therefore, not surprising.

Have you ever been touched by a fleeting glimpse of joyful heart and peaceful mind? It comes from this domain. When you meet a loved one, the mind stops for a while and this eternal source of bliss becomes available, though only for a moment. That is joy. But the window closes quickly and the experience abates much like lightening that hits the thunderstorm for split second. There is light all around and the hidden landscape is revealed. But it is soon lost as the darkness engulfs again. This space (the word space is being used for want of a better one) is the silence that resides in you. It is not the silence that people practice. It is there by itself – never offended or disturbed because there is no 'you' there. There's no one trying to be silent, no one practicing to be quiet. It simply is – beyond any doing.

While 'Making You Turn' in the right direction and unlocking the door to this eternal silence, GRAF can connect us with our very own true nature – something that can only be known through personal experience.

## SILENCE SINGS MY SONG

*To be part of the whole*
*To love you with my soul*
*I rise and evolve*
*I learn and resolve*
*To let go*
*From holding to releasing*
*From gushing to flowing*
*From binding to unleashing*
*From a cocoon to expanding*
*Showering and quenching*
*Plunging deep and yet*
*Surfacing to get*
*Under your wings*
*Where I am secure*
*I ripen and mature*
*With your grace*
*I sense an early trace*
*Of a shift*
*In the deepest of my core*
*I need no more*
*The braces of the words*

*Or the music of the birds*
*In your divine love*
*As I yearn and long*
*The silence sweetly*
*Sings my song.*

(A poem from the book **"Till I become you"** by Harkirat)

# THE TOOL BOX

## Chapter 10

# THE TOOL BOX

Reader must have noticed the thematic trajectory this book traces. It mirrors a shift from external chaos to internal calm, aided by navigators namely, Gratitude, Responsibility, Acceptance and Forgiveness. We reiterate, even at the risk of sounding repetitive, that each constituent of GRAF is not meant to be understood merely as an academic concept. Reading about the power of GRAF, listening to arguments about need to propagate it or watching creative videos that illustrate its efficacy in transforming life will not make any difference to the way we experience life. It is only when the understanding about GRAF is internalized and assimilated, that it becomes an inseparable part of our existence – much like our evolutionary default responses. That helps us in taking control of our lives, rather than being controlled by emotions be it anger, jealousy, hatred, resentment, guilt or shame. The old patterns of thinking and responding change bringing a greater sense of openness, joy and fulfillment. Newer ways of perceiving and behaving start emerging. The possibility of this transformation arises when we move from knowledge to knowing. The question is – how would it happen?

The first step is to understand GRAF as a concept. A diligent study of the earlier chapters of this book will certainly help you. Our experience shows that the most effective way to delve deeply in the content is by reading it in a group of eight to ten likeminded persons. We also strongly recommend that both husband and wife should participate in such group reading. Their togetherness in this endeavor makes continuous learning possible. They can constantly remind each other to use all opportunities of practicing GRAF in daily family life situations. The second step is to daily practice certain exercises which enable us to know GRAF at the level of feeling. So it is a matter of both the head and the heart. Choose to practice a technique that resonate with you the most. The physical act inherent in a particular exercise is important, but the intended outcome depends solely on how well you act them out emotionally.

In most of the techniques mentioned below, breath is involved in some or the other way. All over the world, the monks living in monasteries practice these techniques for years with deep commitment, yet they report repeated failure. So, do not be disheartened when you fail.The issue is not to judge how well you practiced or what experience it brought, but to be mindful of what is happening without preferring one outcome over the other.

Start your practice by silently repeating a prayer in your heart. It can be:

"I devote myself fully to this practice. May it help me experience the beauty of life energy."

## Technique-1

**Objective:** To spend exclusive time with oneself

**Outcome:** A sense of relaxation and quietness that recharges

Fix a particular place in your house. Keep some time apart from daily chores when you can sit (either on a mat or in a chair) in a relaxed state. Keep your spine straight. Close your eyes and take few deep breaths. Become aware of your body starting from top of the head and ending at the toes. In whichever part of the body you find tension, just relax it mindfully.

Watch your breath go in and come out. You will be distracted by thoughts (inner chatter) and may even be carried away by them.

As soon as you realize this has happened, go back to the breath.

It would be useful if you do it for at least 10 minutes every day.

This practice can also be repeated quietly anywhere and at any time for short durations say a minute or so.

### Technique-2

**Objective:** To increase the flow of energy in the heart

**Outcome:** The emotional state shifts to a higher level.

Stage-1

Keep your eyes closed and take a deep breath. Visualize your heart (the area located in the middle of the chest where people absentmindedly keep their hand when they express their love) opening just like a bud opens to become a flower. Relax and release the breath.

- Tell yourself that no matter what happens going forward or has already happened, you will not let the heart close. Relax and release the breath.
- Do not react to thoughts about people or situations that may appear in your mind. Don't let likes and dislikes bother you during this exercise. Let go of them. Relax and release the breath.

Stage-2

- Exhale as deeply as you can, while at the same time visualizing that all negativities within are being thrown out with the air you are exhaling.
- Let the lungs be empty as much as possible. After exhalation is complete, stop for as long as you can. Then let the air rush back and fill you up, while simultaneously visualizing your heart opening up like a flower.

Repeat this cycle at least ten times. This can be done any time in the day and is effective when you feel negativities like sadness, worry, jealousy, resentment. It will help in washing them away while lifting your mood.

### Technique-3

**Objective:** To acknowledge the gifts routinely overlooked

**Outcome:** Gratitude becomes a way of life

There are innumerable things and situations which are taken for granted. We grow so used to their presence that we appreciate their significance only when they are denied. To understand this do the following activities:

- Make a list of things, people and events that have helped you in your life
- Think of difficult times you have been through and look for the lesson they might have taught
- Notice the furniture, computer and other things in the room. Slowly examine how they have contributed in making your life easy.
- You can breathe, walk, talk, eat and sleep. Imagine if you could not? Is this not good fortune?

## Technique-4

**Objective:** To accept "what is"

**Outcome:** Inner disturbances settle

Picture yourself in the future, years from now, in a very peaceful and safe place far away from your existing environment. The sun is shining, there is a pleasant gentle breeze and you are calm about everything.

This is a thought experiment which allows you to move into a new phase of life. Now look back at what is bothering you in life today. You are trying to see the present from a future date. A new perspective emerges and the situation which is causing overwhelming disturbance might look less intimidating. To overcome it further, shrug your shoulders, smile gently and say "It was just one of those things."

## Technique-5

**Objective:** To accept yourself

**Outcome:** Enhanced self-esteem

We must learn to accept our body, thoughts and emotions as they are.

**5.1** Stand before a looking glass and smile. Say, "I love you, dear. Don't worry? It will be all right." It is not easy but it will definitely make you more aware of your own words and they will sink to a deeper level than ever before. When something good happens in your life, go to the mirror and say, "Thank you! Thank you for doing this." If something bad happens, you can go to the mirror and say, "This will pass, but I love you as you are."

For most of us, facing the mirror is difficult at first. But with persistent effort you become less self-critical.

It takes only a second to say, "Hi!" or "Looking good" or "Isn't this fun? Cheer up." It's very important to give yourself small but positive messages throughout the day.

**5.2** At any time in the day, whatever the mood be, sit comfortably and let your jaw drop. Let the mouth open slightly and also let the body breathe on its own. Do not make any effort to deep breathe. It will gradually become shallow and the body will relax. Focus on the area around the navel and imagine a smile arising from it. This is not the same smile that comes on the face but it is the one in which the entire being smiles. It is not confined to the lips but comes from deep within. Be very sensitive to it because if at any time, you stop being attentive to the presence of this smile, it will quickly fade away. But it is something which can be felt as it spreads all over the body. This smile gives an experience of what it feels like to completely accept oneself.

### Technique-6

**Objective:** Forgiving others

**Outcome:** Hurts get healed

**6.1** This exercise should preferably be done immediately before going to sleep at night. Sit in your bed. Close your eyes and relax. Take few deep breaths. Now recall the incident in which you had felt hurt in details. Identify clearly the actions that wronged you. As you would go back in the memory lane feelings will start arising. They will be the same feelings which you had felt at the time of the incident. The story of grievance may start playing in the mind. The pain of the incident will come back. Just experience all the sensations that arise without modifying them in any way. Do not resist anything. If your mind shifts to some new thought process, go back to the sensations which the experience of recalling the incident gave birth to.

This process will bring you in close contact with the pain. It is actually reliving the pain. Notice whether over time the exercise reduces the intensity of pain or not.

**6.2** Make a daily ritual of recalling the events of the day before going to sleep. Seek apology from all those who came in contact during the day. Don't pick and choose people because you may have hurt some without even knowing it. The apology must come from the heart and not be just another habit.

### Technique-7

**Objective:** Modifying the mental patterns

**Outcome:** A peaceful mind

- Remember the doctor who treated your sickness and be thankful
- Identify all the people who contribute in bringing food to your table
- Seek forgiveness from someone you hurt
- Recall the moments when your mother lovingly caressed you
- Visualize the beautiful sunset that you had once watched.

- Feel the breath as it goes in and out for a minute. Realize that you are alive because of it. Say thank you to the breath.

Do such things as many times as possible during the day – while travelling, waiting or by taking a pause while doing work. It is an attempt to look at good things in life so that the predominant tendency of the mind to remain preoccupied with 'what is missing' is minimized.

## Technique-8

**Objective:** To stay in the present moment

**Outcome:** Freedom from worries of the future and regrets of the past

When you are doing something say reading, working on computer, cleaning, eating – pause for moment. Just discontinue what you are doing. Sit with ease, close eyes, take a few deep breaths. With each exhalation let go of any

1. Worry or thought about what you are going to do next;
2. Any tightness in the body.

Be sensitive to whatever is being experienced—sensations in the body, anxiety or restlessness in the mind, mental stories, wanting to resume the activity etc.

Pause is sacred. You can include it in daily routine for few moments at regular intervals or when you begin and end particular activities. You can pause while sitting, standing or lying down or moving. You can pause internally keeping your eyes open and senses awake. You begin life afresh after the pause.

You can experiment by choosing one thing you do daily and make a week long commitment to pause before beginning this activity. It can be anything – bathing, making phone call, stepping into lift, turning on your computer.

Pause can also be at times mixed with Stop. This means to just freeze at any moment when you are free to do it. You are standing – say 'stop'. Now don't move. Let the body stay in the position in which it heard STOP. With closed eyes feel the body. Stay for as long as you can.

This exercise is best done at random. This can be practiced anywhere and anytime and does not require any preparation.

### Technique-9

**Objective:** To drop a habit mindfully

**Outcome:** Freedom from habits you want to change

This exercise can be done at anytime of the day and anywhere when free for few moments. Bring your attention to anything that you want compulsively. It can be anything like food, smoking, alcohol, sex, judging others, computer gaming or rising late in the morning. Pause and become physically still, paying close attention to this feeling of wanting. What is happening in the body in the presence of this desire? In which part of the body do you experience the sensation of wanting the most? Watch. It can be felt as craving in the stomach, heaviness in the chest, aching in the arms. Check if your mind is chattering or sluggish. Notice if your experience changes during the pause. Ask if you are still missing what was wanted as acutely as it was earlier?

If after the pause you still move into the act of fulfilling the want, do so slowly and mindfully. Keep noticing clearly and compassionately the sensation, emotion and thoughts that arise during the act.

## Technique-10

**Objective:** To feel oneness with your partner

**Outcome:** Intimacy in relationship will improve

This may be done only at night. Sit facing each other in a relaxed environment. Keep the lights low.

First step:

Cross your arms and hold each other's hands – right hand in the right and left in the left hand of the partner. Look into each other's eyes directly. Keep your eyes comfortably open. Blink normally without removing the gaze. Don't let go of hands whatever may happen. Let the body sway the way it wants.

Second step:

Both of you close your eyes and sway your body. Keep hands as in stage one.

Third step:

Now stand and sway together. Keep eyes closed and hands held as before in stage one.

Each stage must last for at least 5 minutes.

### Technique-11

**Objective:** To detoxify mind-body complex

**Outcome:** Deep calmness within

There are social, cultural or familial compulsions or conditionings which stop us from expressing what comes to mind in a given moment. This happens very frequently as we engage with other people. It is necessary to purge system of these pent up emotions. Choose a time and place where privacy is possible. Now speak out whatever comes to mind without caring about its purpose, implications, meaning or rationality. Use structure and sound of human language – but don't use your vocabulary. Don't use the language you know.

Also do not grunt or growl. So scream, shout and vent your feelings in words that make no sense in terms of vocabulary. It is like using a language that is only known to you.

Do it for 10 minutes. Now laugh and do it totally. Don't look for a reason to laugh. Just do it. If thereafter you feel like crying, let tears flow. If you prefer to be silent, remain so. Lie down preferably on the floor and be still as if dead, making no effort of breathing. Just be. This technique unburdens the mind.

We have not restricted the scope of techniques mentioned in this chapter to only those which help us directly cultivate GRAF. Most of them aim at restoring inner order which is essential precondition of a joyful life. Try them out over a period of time and identify ones that come naturally to you. They will collectively make your personal toolbox. Use it as often as possible. It would help you to live from the much coveted space of silence.

# About The Authors

Iqbal Singh Bains has served in Indian Administrative Service for over three-and-a-half decades.

Dr Harkirat Bains is a Professor with the Indira Gandhi National (Open) University. Her published works include: *The Last Autumn Leaf*, *Till I Become You* and *Wohi Mera Khuda Hoga*, all collections of her poems.

# Acknowledgement

We acknowledge, at the outset, that this book is an embodiment of the collective effort of many minds, who met over last few years, helping us in many ways to finalize the contents. It is indeed difficult to faithfully make a list that includes every name.

In bringing this work to life, numerous iterations happened over the course of reading the manuscript many times over in different groups. With gratitude to everyone who contributed, we are publishing this book – more as trustees of our collective wisdom and less as authors.

# ACKNOWLEDGEMENT